D1558839

# Don't Forget to Remember

**Aviva Haber Levin**

Print ISBN: 978-1-09835-304-9
eBook ISBN: 978-1-09835-305-6

# Dedication

This book has been written to honor my mother, Sally Susskind, and my father, Arnold Susskind, who both survived the Holocaust. To say they are both my heroes would be an understatement. They are my warriors and heroes. They never ever gave up on me.

To my son Sean, whose devotion, loyalty, perseverance, and love, has been an ever present and constant support. He is the keeper of my secrets. I feel like I grew another heart because one heart is not enough to express my love for him.

To my beloved Tammi, my daughter-in-law, who is the daughter I never had. I couldn't love her more if I had given birth to her. She is my dearest friend and confidant and has shown true understanding of my demons.

To my grandchildren Sarah and Sethy. Sarah has such heart, pizzaz, and self-confidence, qualities I long to have had at her age. Sethy, who eventually won't let me call him that, but to me will always be, is kind and sympathetic to all underdogs. He is just a big heart with arms and legs. I have been blessed not only to have them as my beloved grandchildren, but to share their lives on a day-to-day basis. What an amazing gift.

To Mimi Markus who is truly the wings beneath my feet and without whom I could never have come this far and could never have written this book.

# Table of Contents

# Introduction

## Letter to My Parents

Dear Mom and Dad,

This letter is difficult for me to write because my emotions well up when I think about what you have endured throughout your lives and the impact that your experiences have had on us as a family.

I want you to know that I have finally written this book, *Don't Forget to Remember*, to honor and to pass on your legacy of survival and hope. I have wanted to write it for a long time, but the challenges I have faced as an adult prevented me from reaching the clarity that I needed to do it. Finally, years after you have left this earth, I have found the strength and developed the awareness to understand and to put into words the events that shaped our lives. In this book, I hope to show people who are affected by trauma, loss, and tragedy that they can find happiness.

In the pages of this book, I bring to life the stories each of you told me over the years, as well as those I overheard as a child in your conversations with your survivor friends. These stories show your strength, courage, and persistence in overcoming the unrelenting obstacles you confronted on a daily basis in your fight to live. The Holocaust robbed you of many years of joyful living; you suffered unspeakable losses of your child, your families, and your health. Putting these stories in writing has been painful, bringing back the fear, horror, and anger that I felt when I heard them throughout my life. However, now, as a second generation survivor, I feel that it is my responsibility to share your personal accounts of your experiences with current and future generations.

You have always been my heroes. After we came to America by boat from Bergen-Belsen Displaced Persons Camp, you made a good life for us with hard work and perseverance. As a family, we were devoted and committed to laugh and cry together and always support each other even when sometimes one of us didn't understand. Family and love were the medicine and the glue that held us together until you died in your late nineties.

Your strength, humility, and generosity to others have affected my life deeply. I love you both and miss you, but more importantly, I realize with each passing day that the way you lived your lives has affected me in a positive way. Although you lived a long life filled with great pain, courage, and determination, you always kept hope and joy as your signature of how day-to-day life should be led, no matter what.

Mom, you were so wise and kind, a friend and confidant to all. I think of you every day and quote you all the time. When I had problems with friends and sometimes felt that they weren't being kind as I was to them, it was you, Mom, who would say to me, "Avivala, if you want a friend, you have to close one eye. If you want to have a good friend, you have to close both eyes." I have shared your remarkable words of advice, encouragement, and wisdom with many people, and although they have not had the privilege of knowing you, they wish they could have met you. In many ways, you are my inspiration. If I could have half the wisdom and grace you possessed, I would be a rich woman.

At times, I may have not listened to your advice out of stubbornness, but I recall one time when I followed your intuition, which I like to call your radar, that prevented a tragedy from happening. When Sean was a baby, you often offered to babysit, which I greatly appreciated. One Saturday, Steve, who worked for a department store, had to attend an event to check out the set-up of new merchandise. I always insisted on going with him, and on this occasion, we took Sean with us. On that rainy day, we decided to visit you on our way to the event. I'll never forget how you implored me, "Please don't take Sean. I just had a bad dream last night." Usually, I would have dismissed your request, but this time, I felt the energy of this warning coming through you, so I acquiesced and left Sean with you. As Steve and I were driving to the event in our subcompact Chevy Vega on Sprain Parkway, a narrow, curvy road, a dog suddenly ran across the highway. The drivers of the cars in the lanes next to us instinctively applied their brakes, and all of the cars around us, including ours, started skidding in both directions, ending in a seven-car pile-up. Our car was hit in the back, front, and side. The impact forced Sean's empty car seat to be propelled from the back seat through the front windshield, breaking the glass. Miraculously, not one fatality or major injury occurred. At that moment, I felt that we were all touched by God through you, Mom.

I did not know until you were in your late eighties, Mom, that you missed having a closer relationship with me. With sadness, you made a comment that was a blow to me, one that I will never forget: "I know you love me, but I don't know if you always liked me." I felt regret that I had been so remiss in showing you. Your words inspired me to change my behavior, and over the last seven years of your life, I made living amends to you, showing you how much I both loved and liked you. If you hadn't told me how you felt, I would have missed the opportunity to show my respect and admiration for you.

Your inner strength and perseverance have left an indelible mark on me. Towards the end of your life, Dad and I knew you were in great pain. We could see it in your eyes, but you never complained. In fact, you would always assure us that you would be okay. At the end of your life, the last few moments before you died were the most powerful moments that I have ever spent in your presence. Hospice had been coming to the house for a few days to ensure that you were comfortable. You were frail and had hardly moved for a day, most of the time lying on your side. I knew that you could hear Dad, Helen, who was my parents' care giver, and me because every now and then, as I lay next to you, you squeezed my hand. You were the one who decided when you were leaving us, not the medication. All of a sudden, you, who could not even hold your head up to sip water or eat, lifted yourself up on your elbow with your head resting in your palm. You looked around the room, and with a smile, making eye contact with each of us, told us goodbye with clarity and dignity. It was a moment I'll never forget.

Dad, you were the one I could come to with my secrets, knowing that you would keep a level head no matter what the situation was. You were always the voice of reason. You never judged me for my behavior and my descent into alcohol addiction. I will always appreciate your support as you sat through many recovery program meetings with me.

Dad, over the years, you taught me the virtues of hard work and honesty. I remember how proud you were when after many years managing a shipping department, you were able to buy a business, which gave you great pride. After being held up at gunpoint, you realized that selling the store was your best option. You had to work for someone else again, and I could tell how dejected you felt, but you were determined to make the best of the situation. You found a job in the appliance department at Alexander's. During your breaks, you enjoyed walking around the store because you loved to shop. One day, you were holding several items you wanted to buy when you saw some men's socks on sale. You made your selection and realized that you couldn't hold all of the items in your hands, so you put the socks in your pocket. The security guard thought you were stealing and took you to the office, resulting in your getting fired. When you got home, you put your head down on the kitchen table and sobbed from shame that you had been accused of stealing. When I came home from school and saw you crying, I decided to take matters into my own hands. At the age of fourteen, I went to Alexander's and insisted on speaking to the general manager. I said, "I will not leave this store until he sees me. I will call my school and report you to the school paper if you don't let me see the store manager." When the manager came out, I said, "Do you know who my father is? He is the most honorable, honest man. How did you do this to my father?" I told him that you had survived the Holocaust and gave him examples of your honesty. The manager did apologize to you, and you were able to come back to work. I don't know if you knew what I had done.

One of my deepest regrets, Dad, is not being with you the moment that you died. During the last four years of your life, I had been struggling, having left sobriety. As you approached your ninety-eighth birthday, you were not doing well. I was in a rehab and had made it through twenty-three days when I learned that you were taken to hospice at the JFK Medical Center in Florida. I shared this information with the rehab counselors, who granted me permission to visit you. They felt if anything happened to you, I would never have been able to stay sober. When I arrived at the hospital, you were still alive. You were lucid that day, but by the time I left, you had slipped into a morphine sleep. I spent three days with you until Kenny, concerned that I would miss my outpatient care required by the rehab, wanted me to return to complete the program. He was angry with me because my challenges with sobriety had affected his life for the past few years, and he was afraid that I would drink again. Kenny had given me so many chances, and he couldn't handle it anymore. Yet you, my beloved father, were dying.

As I sat by your bedside, I kept whispering, "Daddy, it's okay to go. I'm okay. Go be with Mommy." But you wouldn't. Being so newly sober and emotionally fragile, I didn't know what to do. I wanted to please Kenny, yet I wanted to be with you, your only child. I asked your nurse what I should do. She took me aside and said, "He may not die if you're here. Sometimes people hold on so as not to die in front of their loved ones." I made the decision to leave on the third day of my visit with you, and the next day I spoke to you while Sean held the phone to your ear. My last words to you were that I loved you and that it had been an honor and a privilege to have been your daughter. That night, I received a call from hospice informing me that you had died at 3 a.m. To this day, I regret that I allowed other people's opinions influence me to do what was unnatural for me. If this had happened today, my choices would have been different.

In my own way, I am a survivor too. This book describes my challenges and struggles with alcoholism and my arduous road to recovery. I know you were not aware of all the drinking I did starting at age thirteen; you were so confused by my behavior. As I grew older, you witnessed my continuing battle with alcoholism. With all the stress and worry I caused you, you supported me. So many times I scared you, but neither one of you gave up on me. When I was drunk, I used to blame you both for all that was wrong with me. I always regretted that I said things to hurt you on purpose because I was hurting so badly. I am forever grateful that God selected you as my parents because I would never have had the strength and courage to recover if it were not for both of you. I ask you to please forgive me.

For many years, I have understood how surviving the Holocaust affected you and how that experience influenced your behavior as parents raising me. Growing up in the shadow of the Holocaust was painful for me, but I realize that you had no one to help you process the trauma you went through, and, as a result, you did the best you could. I have only compassion for what caused you to behave that way.

You have always been my heroes. At some point, when I made the decision to recommit to being sober no matter what life dealt me, no matter how many bowling balls were coming my way, I always told myself that if you could survive the Holocaust, and after the war not know of each other's existence, if you, Mom, could see your son get shot and killed and still remain grateful and hopeful and live life with gratitude and service, then how can I not carry that torch of survival?

I'll never forget to remember. That's what you always said about life. You were my greatest teachers, and I will remember you every day.

# Part 1

## My Parents' Stories

*A*s I was growing up and throughout my adult years, my parents, Sally and Arnold Susskind, told me of their experiences during the Holocaust. They both endured a harsh life in multiple concentration camps, identified not by their names, but by their prisoner numbers. My mother's number, A21538, was tattooed on her arm and remained a constant reminder throughout her life of those dark, traumatic years. My father did not have a tattooed number on his arm, but was identified by different prisoner numbers at each of the nine concentration camps he had been transported to. Researching his records, I learned that at Gross-Rosen, his prisoner number was 14267, and at Buchenwald, his prisoner number was 133926. That they survived was truly a miracle. Their stories of death, loss, and suffering are deeply rooted in my psyche.

When I think about my parents now, I realize that they were the most humble and grateful people I have met to this day. Our lives weren't easy, but they taught me that although their losses were insurmountable, they always kept a kernel of hope. My parents passed on to me the gift of loving life. It was an honor to be their daughter, and their legacy lives on in my son and grandchildren.

Once you have heard Sally and Arnold Susskind's stories, you will never forget them. The stories I share here are derived from my recollections of the many conversations I had with my parents as they remembered and interpreted the details of their trauma through their personal lenses. The war had separated them, so their experiences over those years are different.

Even though my parents didn't know the other was alive after they had been separated and transported to different camps, each of them performed similar rituals in the camps. For instance, they hoarded their stale bread or raw potatoes. They also held on to their Jewish traditions. On Yom Kippur, even though they were given so little to eat on a daily basis, they still fasted. Neither of them gave up on God completely though they questioned how God could allow such atrocities. Even God could not stop the Nazis because people have free will.

I have attempted to connect the disparate details of their accounts into a cohesive narrative. At times, the stories may seem disjointed or incomplete because of gaps in their recounting or of my own inability to remember every detail. As difficult as it is for me to think about these stories, it is even more difficult to write them.

Through the retelling of my parents' stories, I have chosen to accept the responsibility for transmitting them to current and future generations so that they will understand what hate and intolerance can do.

# Chapter 1

## My Mother, Sally Susskind's Story

My mother was born in Mielec, Poland, on October 15, 1915. Mielec is near Krakow, a city in southern Poland. At that time, the population of Mielec was comprised of approximately 6,000 Poles and 6,000 Jews. She lived with her parents, two brothers, Nathan and Leo, and two sisters, Rachel and Bela. My mother didn't share much about her childhood, her parents, and her siblings, perhaps because speaking of them brought back such painful memories.

My mother was the middle child. She adored her parents, but she especially loved her father. Her father had a successful taxi service, providing a good income for the family. Recalling that he hired Polish drivers triggered strong, negative emotions from her: "I like to forget Poland. There's a lot of heartache in this."

Growing up in Poland was not easy for my mother. As a matter of fact, she didn't like to think about it or talk about it because anti-Semitism permeated the lives of all Jews. She said, "I hate to remind myself about it. You can say nothing good about Poland." As a child, she encountered constant prejudice in school and on the street. In public school, the Jewish children were taunted by the Polish children, who called out to them, "You zhyd. Why don't you go to Palestine? You don't belong here." The Jewish children were so adversely affected by this prejudice that they were ashamed to speak Yiddish outside of the house; they had to speak Polish. They even pretended that they didn't know Yiddish.

My mother married my father in 1938. According to her, both sides of the families loved each other and got along well. At that time life was relatively simple and "beautiful." Two months before the war, she gave birth to a boy, Emusch (Evan). The three of them lived with her parents, and she recalled how happy they were. My mother's and my father's parents doted on Emusch. My mother was a dressmaker, and a good one at that. Little did she know that her ability as a dressmaker would actually end up saving her life later on.

One amusing anecdote my mother shared was learning to cook as a new married woman. She had not learned to cook, but she wanted to please my father and decided that she would attempt to make meatloaf. She went to the butcher to buy meat and asked the butcher how to prepare the meatloaf. He told her to add salt and pepper, bread, and egg. She wrote the instructions down, and eager to cook for the first time, she rushed home. When she arrived home, she was suddenly perplexed. Making another trip to the butcher, she asked him earnestly, "Which do you add first? The salt or the pepper?" The butcher chuckled and told her it didn't matter. In time, she became a good "Yiddisha" cook.

Before the war, although my mother and her family began to realize that the situation in Poland wasn't good with a possible war on the horizon, they didn't want to leave the country because they didn't believe that the situation would get so bad for the Jews. Besides, they didn't have anywhere to go. My father had always wanted to go to Israel, but at that time, the English were not accepting Jews in Palestine, so they stayed in Poland. Nobody believed that Hitler would invade and systematically kill all the Jews. They had heard talk that there might be a war, but no one believed that the war would completely change their lives. Then, as if she had begun to relive this moment, my mother explained that the unthinkable and unimaginable started to happen. The German soldiers invaded Poland by air and by land. The war had begun. German troops conquered the cities and began their search for Jews.

The Germans came to Mielec in September 1939 and occupied the town. The soldiers came by motorcycles, planes, and trains. People became fearful because no one knew what the Nazis were going to do. On the eve of Rosh Hashanah, the Jewish people went to their synagogues to pray. They had no idea that the German SS men were embarked on a mission to kill as many Jews as possible. The SS men knew that the Jews in Mielec would be in the synagogue praying, so they poured gasoline on the synagogue, lit it on fire, and watched as the building burned with all the worshippers inside. After this slaughter happened, all the Jews were afraid to leave their homes. The Nazis broke in any time, day or night, and confiscated people's property: clothing, fur coats, whatever they could find. My mother explained how they lived in terror every day, fearing what would happen next.

Once the Germans occupied Mielic, the lives of the Jewish population changed dramatically. Every house was required to have a Jewish star in the window so that the Germans knew where the Jewish families lived. As Jews were identified, they were taken away or killed, their businesses looted and closed. In fact, tragically, her brother Nathan was killed right away. Education stopped for Jewish children because they weren't allowed to go to school. A mandate that all Jews over six years of age had to wear a yellow Star of David on their clothing at all times when they were in public added to the humiliation. Inside of the star, the word "Jew" had to be inscribed in German or the local language. Not long after, the yellow star aided the Nazis in their efforts to segregate the Jews into ghettos and later deport them.

My parents realized that they were in a bad situation, but there was no way of avoiding it. My mother told me that they weren't allowed to leave the country. All of the towns were in the same predicament, so there was no point running to another town. Although some people escaped to Russia, she didn't want to leave her parents. They all did what they could to survive, selling their jewelry so that they could buy food to eat.

My father ran away to the Russian border with her brother and two of her other friends in 1939, leaving my mother and the rest of her family in

Mielec, which was on the German side of the border. At that point, she lost contact with the two of them and didn't know where they were. Then, she heard that my father was in Przemysl where a ghetto had been established. She tried everything she could to run away to Przemysl, but she was not able to because Jews weren't permitted to travel by train. They believed that the occupation would end soon, but sadly they realized that it wasn't going to happen.

In March of 1942, Mielec became *judenfrei*, meaning "clean of Jews," a Nazi term. All of the Jews were deported from Mielec. At three o'clock in the morning, the SS soldiers pounded on the doors and windows of people's homes, waking everyone up. Then, they were taken to a large airplane hangar and held there for several days without being given any food to eat. This was the beginning of their mistreatment and the realization that the situation was going to get worse. My mother explained the fear and dread everyone experienced when each day, the SS carried out what was called "selection." People were separated into groups: those who could work and, therefore, would live, and those who were older or sick, who would be killed. They took her grandfather right away. Another brother had also been killed immediately, and she didn't know where her other brother was. Most of her family members, her mother, father, two sisters, one brother, and a cousin, were deported to Lubyanka. One of her sisters had tried to run away with a cousin, but the SS men killed her at the station in Lublin. My mother and her parents were taken to Lublin on their way to Treblinka, the death camp. Her family had lost their home and had been separated. By this time, my mother wept, remembering that she had lost everything.

Determined to escape, my mother and her cousin realized that they had to leave immediately, knowing they might be caught. She desperately wanted to find my father in Przemysl. My mother was able to acquire false papers identifying her and her cousin as Christian nuns so that they could travel. At one of the stops on the train, she had a harrowing interaction with a Polish policeman, which almost jeopardized her trip. He confronted her:

"You are Jewish." My mother insisted, "No, I'm not Jewish. Don't say this to me." He asked for her papers, which she gave him to read. Judging from the way he looked at the papers, she sensed that he couldn't read. When he handed the papers back to her, she said, "Next time, don't do that to me because I am not Jewish." Relieved, she was glad that the interrogation didn't go any further, for under her shawl, she wore a shirt that had a Jewish star sewn on it, as was required for all Jews. She felt very lucky that she wasn't caught. Finally arriving in Przemysl, which had been converted to a ghetto, she was reunited with my father and his family for a few months.

Day to day existence in the Przemysl ghetto was uncertain. Every day the Nazis took people away and killed them, so my mother, father, and their baby hid in a bunker. A doctor was hiding with them, and my father and he became good friends. One of the Jewish policemen who worked for Schwammberger, the commandant of the ghetto, knew they were hiding. He told them that Schwammberger requested that a doctor be brought to the ghetto and asked if the doctor would come. He would be permitted to bring a friend as his assistant. The doctor asked my father to come along, and he agreed, thinking he would find a way to get my mother out. My mother was left behind in the bunker with her baby, terrified and not knowing what would happen to her. Several days later, my father returned with a wagon filled with wood. He put my mother and the baby on the wagon, placing the wood on top to hide them, and took them to a small ghetto of ninety people.

They lived in that small ghetto, which was part of Przemysl for a short time, and it was there that my mother experienced an unimaginable tragedy. Six of the children in the ghetto had been taken away, and the parents didn't know where. Having her son with her offered some solace, but suddenly the unthinkable happened. Weeping bitterly, my mother recounted the story. For no reason at all except that my baby brother Emusch was crying, one soldier got angry, and he shot and killed Emusch right in front of my mother. She told me that she found it too difficult to talk about and claimed that she had repressed her memory of that event. I'm not sure that she ever recovered.

The next day, the people in the ghetto were told they would be taken to another camp, this time in Krakau. Some of the women didn't want to go; they didn't want to live anymore because they thought that they were going to die anyway. The night before they were to leave, some of the women, eight or nine according to my mother, poisoned themselves. When everyone heard what had happened, they were devastated.

The passage of time was immeasurable; they had no way to determine the time, the day, or the months. According to my mother, the morning after those women had committed suicide, either in September or October of 1942, my mother and the others were sent to Plaszow, a concentration camp. They were forced to live in a crowded barracks with as many as four bunks stacked above one another. Life in this camp was terrible, and my mother remarked that living there was difficult, and while I knew it caused her distress to talk about it, I urged her on. They were given very little to eat. Breakfast was a cup of weak black coffee and a piece of bread. Lunch was a small portion of watered down soup, although she was grateful that it was warm at least. The women were given uniforms to wear and forced to go to work. Each day, the Germans woke them up at three o'clock in the morning, requiring them to stand outside the barracks to be counted. In lines five deep, they stood barefooted for three or four hours in all weather conditions: rain, snow, and freezing temperatures. After the initial count had been completed, another officer would count them again. My mother emphasized that the experience was "absolutely terrible. It wasn't so easy." This counting routine was performed every day because many people tried to run away. Those who managed to run away were found and killed. In addition to these hardships was the ever present, horrid smell of bodies burning in the ovens that permeated the camp; they had no choice but to get used to it. This odor hung over the camp like a shroud and for some, a harbinger of what could come.

At this camp, many of the women were assigned to work as seamstresses mending the German soldiers' uniforms. Each morning they went to the shop to sew. When they arrived, they were given garments to repair, which were counted at the beginning and end of the workday. For example, she told me that if they were given a dozen pairs of pants, they could cut the fabric from one pair to make patches to repair the others, but they had to give eleven back. If one item was missing, they would be killed right away.

In the beginning of 1943, the women were taken from Plaszow to Auschwitz-Birkenau, a concentration and extermination camp. In order to identify the "prisoners," numbers were tattooed on their arms. My mother rolled up her sleeve to show me the number on her arm, A21538. "You were not a person. You were a number," she lamented. When they arrived there, everything was taken away from them. That night, their hair was cut off. My mother felt fortunate that at least she was with her cousin. The next morning, when they woke up and stood outside to be counted, she remarked that she and her cousin didn't recognize each other without their hair. Because their clothes had been taken, they were given dresses that were torn, revealing parts of their bodies, which embarrassed my mother. The same counting procedure, which went on for several hours, was conducted every day at three o'clock in the morning. She clearly remembers how one of the female guards used to run through the lines to straighten them out, yelling, "Stay in the line. Stay in the line." Sadly, after a few days, my mother's cousin was sent away, another great loss. My mother survived in Auschwitz a few months.

Every day, the women were sent out to work, cleaning the streets, the toilets, and the hospital. "Never in my life I washed a floor. I didn't know how to clean the streets, but you learn to clean the streets. They sent us every day to we didn't know where," my mother explained. In the evening, when they were brought back to the camp, they were counted again and then sent back to their barracks. No beds were provided, so they slept on the straw covered floor with barely any room to move. The barracks had no bathrooms, so if they needed to get up in the middle of the night to relieve themselves, they had to go outside, stepping over those who were sleeping.

My mother shared one specific incident that almost cost her life. Because she knew how to sew, one of the female SS officers asked her to mend and wash some of her clothes, but warned my mother not to get caught. She brought her clothes to my mother secretly so no one would know. The SS woman needed my mother, so she was good to her. To show her gratitude, she often brought my mother an extra piece of bread but cautioned my mother not to tell anyone about it. My mother's friends knew though, because they saw her sewing the officer's items, and sometimes my mother wasn't sent out to work. One morning during the counting procedures, the female SS whispered to my mother that someone had heard about the extra piece of bread she had given my mother and had reported it to the SS men. She warned that the SS men were going to check my mother. If they caught her with the bread, they would kill her. My mother grabbed her piece of bread and gave it to the woman standing next to her, so when the SS men checked her, she had nothing on her, and they let her go.

On another occasion, my mother was beaten. She was afraid of being selected, a process regularly conducted by the SS doctors to remove those who were sick or weak and have them killed. She didn't want to look pale and weak, so she and a friend found a piece of red paper, dampened it with water, and put the dye from the paper on their cheeks and lips. An SS woman thought the color was lipstick and beat my mother, saying, "You need lipstick?"

My mother told me that there were times when the women were willing to take risks because they were starving, as in her story about how she tried to steal extra soup. Every day, a group of women were sent to the kitchen to bring soup to the barracks to feed the prisoners. They carried the heavy pot with enough soup to feed exactly one cup to each of the thirty women in the barracks. Since soup was the only form of nourishment for dinner, the women were always hungry. As the women carrying the heavy pot passed by, my mother would try to dip her cup into the soup, but they would hit her because they knew that they would be blamed if there wasn't enough soup for everyone. On one occasion, she grabbed two cups of soup, drank it quickly, and as a result, got sick to her stomach. She lay outside, afraid to say that she didn't feel well and promising herself never to do that again.

In the beginning of 1944, the women were sent from Auschwitz in wagons without any food for the long trip to Bergen-Belsen. Bergen-Belsen was an army camp, "no better or worse than Auschwitz," according to my mother. They were given striped uniforms to wear. In her words, "We didn't have beds. Was raining or cold, nobody there cared." They slept on straw on the floor, got up early in the morning for counting, and were sent to work. In this camp, once again, my mother fixed the uniforms for the soldiers. Here my mother saw terrible things: people dying from hunger and disease.

The days dragged on, and no one in the camp knew that liberation was coming. A few days before the liberation, my mother had contracted typhoid fever and was very sick, too delirious to understand what was happening. When she was told about the liberation, her delirium prevented her from believing it. Several days later, she found out that the English had liberated the camp on April 15, 1945. Sadly, all of her friends had died. My mother remembers that, finally, she and several other women were given a room with four beds, a comfort that they had been denied for so long. They had survived.

Four or five months after the liberation, people wanted to find out if any of their loved ones had survived. My mother and a friend decided to go to her hometown, Mielec, to look for my father and her relatives. In her heart, she knew they weren't alive, but she just didn't want to believe it. She said, "Sometimes you're so hurt inside. When a family loses one person, it's a big tragedy, right? When you lose everybody in one time, when you find out that so many people from your family were not alive, I couldn't believe it."

The three-week trip to Mielec was a difficult one, especially for my mother who was in a weakened condition, not only from having had typhoid fever, but also from having been starved for so long. She and her friend traveled by train, riding on top of open rail cars that were carrying food supplies. Recalling the precariousness of that trip, she told me how frightened they were because whenever the train changed direction, they almost fell off. Once in Mielec, she found her cousin Sigmund, who told her that very few Jewish people were left in the town. She asked him to take her to her parents' former home. When she saw the home, memories or her former life rushed in, upsetting her so much that she fainted. Adding to her distress, they encountered one of her father's former Polish employees who, upon seeing her, remarked with hatred, "You're still alive? I thought Hitler killed all of them." As she told me about this incident, she broke down and cried. After this interaction with him, she insisted that Sigmund take her to his home. Although she remembered that her family had hidden some gold in the house before the family was forced out, she was too upset to look for it. Sigmund offered to sell any property left by her parents, grandparents, and brother, but my mother refused; she didn't want anything. She told Sigmund, "I don't want to stay here. I don't want anything!" She insisted on returning to her cousin's house.

Another unnerving incident occurred when my mother and Sigmund went back to his house. As they were sitting at the kitchen table, all of a sudden, someone hurled a rock through the window. The trauma of having faced the possibility of imminent death in the camp was still very much alive in her mind. My mother interpreted this event as an attempt by someone who was trying to kill her. Terrified, she said, "I went through Hitler! I lived through Hitler! Now I have to lose my life here?" Her cousin tried to soothe her, but she was determined to leave immediately.

Although my mother's visit to Mielec was filled with sadness, the trip gave her a glimmer of hope for her long yearned for reunion with my father. They had been sent to different concentration camps, separated from each other for about five years. Somehow, they learned that the other was alive, but as my mother tells it, their reunion was delayed by a somewhat comical series of events, though she found it quite frustrating at the time. Ironically, they had missed each other at the train station in Bergen-Belsen. My mother had heard that my father had gone to Mielec to look for her, so she was waiting at the station for the train to take her there. At the same time, my father, who had been in Mielec and heard that she was in Bergen-Belsen, was returning to the same railroad station. When she arrived in Mielec, my father had already gone. It took three weeks for her to return to Bergen-Belsen where my parents were finally reunited and started a new life.

After my parents found each other, they lived in the displaced persons camp at Bergen-Belsen. Although many survivors went to the United States in 1947 and 1948, they decided to stay. My parents got paying office jobs. Support for the survivors was supplied by the American Jewish Joint Distribution Committee (JDC) and the United Nations Relief and Rehabilitation Administration (UNRRA).

My mother smiled when she reminisced about my birth on April 7, 1947. The new life that my parents had created was a symbol of their hope for the future. She chose my name, Aviva, which was derived from the Hebrew word *aviv*, meaning spring, because they had been liberated in April. They also wanted me to have a Hebrew name since they thought they were going to settle in Israel.

My parents' plans to go to Israel were hindered by a weak economy in Israel at that time and my father's back problems. My mother explained that my father had been suffering from a dislocated disk, preventing him from walking. If he didn't have surgery, he would end up in a wheelchair. Because my father didn't want to upset my mother, he arranged for the surgery in Eppendorf Hospital in Hamburg without telling her. Instead, he told her that he would be going out of town for a few days to see a doctor about his back problem and that she wouldn't be able to call him because the telephones would be disconnected. She didn't believe him because she knew that Eppendorf was the biggest hospital in Germany and would have many telephones. Eventually, she called a friend of theirs whom my father had told about the surgery, and at her insistence, he took her to the hospital where she learned that he had already had the operation and was recovering.

My parents and I finally came to the United States in July 1950. "We thanked God we survived. It was difficult, but we survived. When your father and I go, I want my grandson and my daughter to talk about this. They should remember this. We are the last ones, the survivors. We want the world to know what Hitler did to the Jewish people. We should never forget. Never. Never. Never."

Concentration Camps where my mother was imprisoned during the Holocaust:

- Bergen-Belsen (Germany)
- Krakau-Plaszow (Poland)
- Auschwitz (Poland)

# Chapter 2

## My Father, Arnold Susskind's Story

$\mathcal{M}$y father was born in Przemysl, Poland, on August 22, 1910. Przemysl is a city located in southeastern Poland. He described it as a beautiful area with the San River running through the middle of the city. The town connected the mountains on one side to the lowlands on the other. The population was about 96,000 then, consisting of Poles, Ukrainians, and Jews. About one-third of the population was Jewish.

His father, Pincus, and his mother, Helen, had four children, two boys and two girls. My father was the oldest child. They lived on the tenth floor of an apartment building. On the ground floor, his father had a confectionary store where he sold imported chocolates and other candies.

As a young adult, my father told me that he dreamed of going to Israel. He realized that the Jews had no future in Poland due to rampant anti-Semitism. Therefore, he became active in Jewish life to prepare to live in Israel. At the age of fifteen, he joined a Zionist movement youth group called Betar, which not only emphasized the Hebrew language, culture, and self-defense, but also had the goal of establishing a Jewish state in Israel. They worked to accumulate funds to send young people to Israel. My father traveled from town to town organizing young people. At seventeen, he qualified for his *hashara*, a Hebrew word meaning preparedness. The troops spent weeks at a time in the woods or mountains, training for any type of battle they might face when in Palestine, which was occupied by the British at that time.

As a member of Betar, he was in charge of the *hashara* group several times. Most of the young boys and girls had never done physical work, so my father had to prepare them. They traveled to places, such as lumber mills and factories, to work. One time, he was sent to Klosow, a village in southwestern Poland. Without his parents knowing, he had run away from school in the middle of the night to work there, although his sister knew. Eventually, he wrote to his parents, telling them where he was. In Klosow, he made cobblestones from granite and other stones. When he returned home after having spent eleven months there, he had become very physically strong from the hard work he had done. After that, he was entitled to go to Israel, but unfortunately, the British closed off the borders and wouldn't let anyone into Israel, so he was stuck in Poland. Instead, he wrote for a newspaper until the war broke out.

Just as my mother did, my father also experienced anti-Semitism. He related one story of how one of his good friends turned against him. In his youth, he had developed a friendship with a Polish Christian boy. They had been good friends for about eleven years, and this friend had frequently spent time at my father's family's home, often having dinner with them. My mother even fixed his clothes because she knew how to sew. When the war broke out, my father went to his friend's house to spend time with him, but the friend turned my father away, speaking with hate, "Get out, you stinking Jew!" That's when my father realized what was coming. He knew it was going to be very bad.

As my father tells it, he fell in love with my mother the first moment he saw her. They were married before the war in 1937, although she insisted it was in 1938. They lived comfortably in her parents' house, and my mother's parents gave my father money to open a stationery store. They were very happy until the Germans invaded. Then the devastation began.

In the beginning of September, my father explained that they realized that the situation was rapidly becoming alarming for the Jews. They had heard talk that war was inevitable, but nobody believed that this war would completely change and destroy their lives. Then, the unimaginable started to happen. The German soldiers invaded Poland by air and by land. The war had begun. German troops conquered Polish cities and began their search for Jews.

First, the SS men confiscated everything. My father remembers how many Jews were forced out of their homes. During the first three months, all the Jews were restricted. For example, they couldn't walk on the sidewalk, only in the streets where the horses walked and defecated. The SS men made the Jews clean the streets, apartments and houses, and collect all of the items the relocated Jews had left behind.

The Jewish people were rounded up from other small towns, forced to leave everything behind, and were brought to my father's hometown, Przemsyl, a small section of which was converted into a walled ghetto. They were ordered to take only those possessions that they could carry and were given a time frame of twenty-four hours to accomplish it. The Jews were not given any food and were not allowed to access markets or medicine. Even more horrifying, the Nazis took the elderly people and small children away and murdered them. Sick people were shot right away. My father's brother, Chaim, who had multiple sclerosis and was not well, was taken away.

The only work those who were healthy were permitted to do was coordinated by the SS, who took them out of the ghetto to various work environments. Fortunately, my father was healthy and avoided being relocated, but when he and the other men had begun their march to work one day, my father was shocked when he saw his mother and sister being taken out of the group. He didn't know at the time why they were selected or what the Germans were going to do with them. The next day, he was devastated when he learned that they had been taken outside of the city into the forest and shot. At this point in the story, remembering the loss of his family members, tears formed in my father's eyes, but he continued, determined to continue with the rest of his story.

Every few weeks, he explained that the ghetto became more crowded as more Jews were brought there, leaving less space for people to live. Towards the end of September, the Germans and Russians split the city of Przemsyl with the San River being the demarcation line. My mother was on the German side, while my father was on the Russian side. They wanted to be together, and my mother took an enormous risk to join him. My father related the same story that my mother did about how she acquired false papers to travel as a Christian nun to be with him. She brought their son, Emusch, and for a while, they were together as a family, but their lives were in danger. The Nazis were eliminating all of the young and sick people, so my father, my mother, Emusch, and four other families went into hiding in a cellar infested with rats and other unwanted creatures. He explained that they had to dig a hole in the cellar to access water, but at the time, they were unaware that the water had high levels of iron, causing some people to lose their teeth. During the months they were hiding, my father was able to use what little money he had to buy bread from a Polish man he knew. When the money ran out, my father insisted that the family needed to take a chance and run away. The timeliness of this desire to leave was confirmed when peering out of their dirty window of the cellar, they saw the gestapo walk past, accompanied by a German shepherd, an ominous sign that something awful was going to happen. They immediately left the cellar, found another bunker, and hid there.

Another chance my father took to try to save his family was the time when he had the opportunity to leave the bunker to be a doctor's assistant. At the time, my parents and three other families were hiding together. A man who had been studying to be a doctor and my father became good friends. Schwammberger, the cruel, sadistic commandant of the ghetto that my parents had run away from, wanted his Jewish policemen to find a Jewish doctor and bring him to the ghetto. One of the policemen, who was sympathetic to the Jews who were hiding and the only one they could trust, knew about the bunker where my father was; he also knew that a doctor was hiding there as well. The policeman asked the doctor to go to the ghetto and to bring an assistant with him, promising that nothing would happen to either of them. Although my father didn't want to leave my mother, she insisted that he go, thinking that he would find a way to help her and the baby. When he arrived at the barracks in the ghetto, he organized a group, paid off two Ukrainians who were working for the Nazis, and obtained a wagon. Then he went back to the bunker, picked up my mother and Emusch, and brought them to the ghetto.

The family was together once again, but another disruption to their lives was about to occur. Schwammberger liquidated most of the Jews in the Przemysl ghetto, leaving one hundred Jews in a building that used to be a soldiers' barracks. They were told to sort all of the items taken from the Jews, such as clothing, gold, silver, and diamonds, which were then sent to Germany. Then, one night in February 1944, the Nazis rounded up all the men and shipped them to the Stalowa Wola forced labor camp, leaving the women and children alone in the ghetto. A few days later, they took all the children and killed them. My father didn't know that his son Emusch had been killed by a Nazi who had been annoyed at his crying. My mother was devastated, not able to do anything to save him.

During the last year of the war, my father was sent from one camp to another to do hard labor. At Stalowa Wola, where about three hundred men were imprisoned, my father worked in a metal factory. Then, one day, the Nazis took all the men to Plaszow, a labor and concentration camp, which is the camp where my mother had been taken. He felt fortunate to be in the same camp as my mother. He learned that she worked in the clothing department fixing the German soldiers' uniforms. When she learned that he was there, she brought him a pair of pants, a shirt, a jacket, and a pair of shoes because he had inadequate, ripped clothing. My parents were glad that they were in the same location and looked forward to seeing each other that night. However, his elation about their reunion was shattered by the events that were to follow. The first day that my father and the other men were brought to that camp, they were beaten. The soldiers told them to go into the shower and pull down their pants. Then, Getz, the camp commandant, beat them for no reason but for his own pleasure. Afterwards, they were put to work moving stones from one place to another, again for no reason except to wear the men down. Unfortunately, my father's stay at Plaszow was only a day and a half, and the next evening, the men were taken in box wagons to Gross-Rosen, while my mother was taken to Auschwitz. The meeting that my parents had planned never happened.

At Gross-Rosen, the men were not accounted for by name, but rather by numbers. My father's prisoner identification number was 14267. The capo at Gross-Rosen was a devil, according to my father. He remembers how the capo stood in a watch tower in the middle of the camp, yelling into a microphone at the prisoners. It was at this camp that my father's gold teeth were ripped out of his mouth with a pliers. Three days later, the men were sent from Gross-Rosen to a series of sub-camps. One of these camps was Hirschberg where the men loaded some heavy, black material, which my father couldn't identify. From there, they were taken to another camp, Dora or Buna, for a short time; he couldn't remember which camp.

Every evacuation from one camp to the other was difficult. He never knew where the SS men were taking him or how long he would be at a particular camp. On one occasion, one of his friends who was succumbing to the bitter cold told my father to take his shoes because my father was barefoot as were many of the men marching. My father did take his friend's shoes, and while others died from untreated frostbite, he did not perish. Remembering his friend's words, my father saved his own life and others by removing the shoes of those who had died. It was difficult, and my father had great misgivings about taking clothes and shoes, but these items kept him and others alive.

My father singled out the march to Buchenwald as the worst of them all. Towards the end of the war, the Germans were instructed to kill any prisoners who could not walk or travel. These evacuations were called Death Marches by the prisoners because many people died on the road or were shot. Hundreds of prisoners died; they were already in a weakened condition from starvation, illness, and beatings, exacerbated by marching for miles in the bitter cold weather. During this march, my father had another brush with death. In the dead of winter, around three thousand men were forced to travel on foot. At this point, my father had been suffering physically from lack of food, overwork, and beatings. On this occasion, a Romanian boy held on to my father because the boy was very weak. Neither of them were strong, but my father wanted to help, so he allowed the boy to lean on him so that together, they could continue marching with the rest of the men. All of a sudden, my father felt a burning sensation in his leg. At that moment, he didn't realize that the SS guard had been shooting at the boy but missed; instead, the bullet pierced my father's flesh. Realizing that he had missed his target, the SS man aimed his gun at the boy a second time and killed him. The Death March continued, and my father, growing increasingly weak from his wound, walked all the way to Buchenwald with blood streaming from his leg. It was a miracle that he made it through the three days and four nights of the march in the rain. His shoes had fallen apart, so he walked barefoot. He told me that he didn't even feel pain. He mused, "I never caught a cold over there. Never got sick. This is a mystery."

Only twelve hundred men survived the Death March. Upon arrival, the remaining men were once again accounted for by numbers, not names. My father became prisoner 133926. He realized that he had to get some medical help for his wounded leg. Although he had heard stories about people who went to the hospital at Buchenwald never came out, he knew he had to take a chance, or he could die. He showed his wound to the German-Jewish doctor at the hospital who told him that gangrene had started to set in, a frightening prospect. The doctor treated the wound, and fortunately, my father survived. However, for the rest of his life, he had problems with that leg.

At Buchenwald, the men continued to be at the mercy of the German soldiers. They were taken to a barrack, a large building that was formerly used as a movie house for the German soldiers. Once again, the men had to cope with more punishment. While they were eating a meager meal of soup and a small piece of bread, suddenly, the soldiers took their food away without explaining the reason. Later my father learned that Leon Blum, a French Jewish political prisoner at the camp, who was the Prime Minister before the war, had been kidnapped by some of the prisoners who were part of the French political underground and saved Blum. The SS men punished everyone for the kidnapping by not giving them any food and then forcing them to run back and forth over stony ground.

Not long after, the men were again forced to march to another camp, Bolkenhain, where punishment always overshadowed their daily lives. It was a small camp of three hundred to four hundred people. To show how little it took to make the men happy, my father remarked that at least the barracks were nice and new. However, the conditions were tough, and they were not given much food to eat. Every morning, the men were awakened at four o'clock and were fed a one-quarter inch slice of bread and what the men called "coffee water," a beverage that was black in appearance but wasn't coffee. For lunch they were given one portion of watery soup, except on Sundays when the soup was heartier.

My father knew that the SS men wanted them to die. As a deterrent, the SS men conducted punishments in the middle of the concentration camp where four large barrels of water were placed. To punish someone, a capo would pick the prisoner up by his legs and put him in the barrel headfirst until he drowned. Sadly, five men from my father's hometown were killed; one had stolen a piece of bread, and another had hidden under the bed instead of getting up for roll call. The SS men always found something to punish them for.

Their work at Boklenhain was difficult, and the men feared being punished for making a mistake. Beatings, freezing cold weather, and starvation were taking their toll on the men. They had to walk four miles to work and back and toil through the night in an airplane factory, making propeller parts on machines. My father received a beating when he accidentally broke a cutter because he had fallen asleep. Every day, when the men came back to the camp from work, they were forced to stand outside so the soldiers could count them. This was especially physically torturous in the winter because they wore only striped uniforms—no underwear, socks, or coats. Some people perished where they were standing. He vividly described one cold, windy day in November when the men were forced to stand outside for five hours; about twenty percent of them succumbed. At one moment, he explained, they were talking, and, suddenly, they fell down and died. After eight or nine months, the men were moved to Dora, a forced labor sub camp where they spent two and a half days doing mining work.

In the early spring of 1945, the men were moved to Buchenwald. One day, the SS men said, "Everyone line up." The men thought that they were going to march to work. To their surprise, each of them was given a half a loaf of bread, marmalade, and cheese, a feast compared to the meager fare that was usually provided. Suddenly, American planes could be seen flying over Buchenwald. The Americans didn't drop bombs on the camp, so the men assumed that they didn't want to hurt them. The SS men realized that the Americans were coming to defeat the Germans and to save the survivors. In a panic, the SS men decided to round up the remaining men and kill them. They called out, "Who wants to march with us?" My father's friend asked him to go, but my father said, "I'm not going no place. They have to shoot me. Let them kill me." He didn't have the strength. He also knew that if he started walking, the SS men would kill him. About six men stayed, while the rest of the men went with the soldiers, who put them in empty wagons and shot them all. "Luck was with me," said my father.

But he wasn't lucky for long. A German soldier came up to him and said, "You still alive?" My father didn't answer. Then the soldier hit him in the face with the butt of a gun. As blood streamed from his face, my father had an idea. He turned over and pretended he was dead. The soldier kicked him in the back saying, "Finally, you stinking Jew. You dead," and walked away. In an act of kindness, a Czechoslovakian boy whom my father had befriended washed the blood off of my father's face.

On a sunny day, April 15, 1945, my father heard the men in the camp yell, "The Americans are here!" Everyone ran to look out of the windows of the barracks. My father told me that he was too weak to get up, but he heard the commotion. The Americans had come to the camp looking for the Germans, but the Germans had run away in fear. The camp had been liberated. My father was in a state of disbelief and bewilderment. He could not process that he was free.

Although my father had survived, he had no strength left. A few American soldiers lifted him up and put him on a straw-covered bed in the barracks. That night, he had his first good night's sleep. The next morning, the American Red Cross came and checked the men to see who was able to walk. The knowledge that my father was free gave him the strength to walk.

Every day, low flying Red Cross aircraft dropped packages of food. All the men had been suffering from malnutrition for many months, even years, and were so hungry that some of them gorged themselves. My father described how his friend, David, whom he had grown close to during their time in the camps, died from eating too much food too quickly. David had grabbed the packages of food that landed on the ground, ripped open one of them, and ate all of the food inside very quickly. His stomach had been empty for such a long time that he became sick and died a painful death. My father was inconsolable from that loss made more tragic because David had survived the Holocaust with all the odds against him only to die from overeating. My father learned to take very small bites of bread over long intervals.

On the third day after the liberation, my father told me that General Eisenhower came to Buchenwald. He shook hands with all of the survivors and watched the American soldiers carry away the bodies of those who had died. Then they took the men who were sick to the hospital. Although my father was weak, he didn't want to go. His previous knowledge of what happened in hospitals in the camps made him fearful. When he received a note from friends in the hospital asking him for some soup, he managed to get some carrots and potatoes from some Germans, put the vegetables in a pot, made a fire, and sat outside in the freezing cold weather waiting for the soup to cook. Shortly after, my father caught a cold that turned into pneumonia, forcing him to seek treatment at the hospital. Although he didn't remember how long he had been in the hospital, he clearly recalled hearing two doctors and a Red Cross person say in German, "If he survives this night, he'll live." The next morning, he woke up and opened his eyes, surprising the medical personnel. Although he had lived through the night, as he described it, "Everything gave up—my hands, my legs." My father lay in the hospital bed for several weeks unable to get up. Finally, the nurses insisted that my father get out of bed to hear Louis Armstrong and his orchestra perform for the survivors at the camp. Several nurses lifted him from his bed to a standing position, and he took his first step, as he remarked, "like a baby." He finally started walking. This was the beginning of his recovery.

After his stay in the hospital, he learned that the Americans and the Russians had split Germany. His camp, Buchenwald, now belonged to the east side that the Russians were given, so everyone had to move out. The Americans asked the men where they wanted to go. Nobody wanted to stay with the Russians. My father decided to go to Poland to look for my mother and the other members of his family.

When my father reached Poland, he learned that the Jewish population had been decimated in his hometown, Przemysl, so instead of going there, he changed his plans and traveled to my mother's hometown, Mielec, to find her. He encountered two families who were her former neighbors and good friends, but they didn't know where she was. Through the Red Cross, he learned that she was alive in Bergen-Belsen, a women's camp in Germany. His desire to travel there was strong, but it wasn't going to be easy. Poland had closed its borders. He knew he would need identification papers to cross the border, but without money, he would not be able to procure them. While traveling by foot to the border, he passed abandoned warehouses that were stocked with a variety of goods left by the German soldiers. People were taking everything they could find. When his eyes fell upon some pieces of leather to make soles for shoes, he realized that the leather was valuable and could be sold, assisting him in his travels to Bergen-Belsen. Placing the pieces of leather in a soldier's bag that he found in the warehouse, he traveled to Krakow where he was able to sell the leather. With the money he received, he bought American five dollar gold coins. Ingeniously, he disguised the coins by placing fabric on top of them so that they looked like buttons. In another stroke of luck, he met a woman from the Red Cross in Krakau with connections to the governor, who helped my father and his friends obtain false identification papers.

My father and his traveling companions didn't realize that they would face many challenges in their attempt to cross the border from Poland to Germany. When they arrived at the Polish border, to their dismay, the guard took all their possessions from them, but fortunately my father's coins, artfully disguised as buttons, were not discovered. The small group successfully crossed the Polish-Czech border in Moravia where they encountered their next challenge, a tall iron bridge "with bumps" as he described it; although traversing it was difficult, my father said they crossed like acrobats. Reaching Czechoslovakia, tired and hungry, they noticed a light in the window of a nearby home in the distance and decided to approach it. A kind Czech family welcomed and fed them a meager fare, which he described as thin sandwiches and a glass of beer. The group couldn't reveal that they were Polish because the Czech people hated the Poles due to Hitler's promise to give Poland part of Czechoslovakia. Instead, my father and his friends identified themselves as German Jews. Although the residents and they spoke different languages, somehow, they communicated. The family told them that a Jewish woman who had survived the war lived ten blocks away and could help them cross the border to Germany. When they went to her home, she generously gave them some food and contacted men she knew who assisted them in reaching the Czech-German border. If they could cross the last border into Germany, they would reach their destination.

At the German border, the group discovered that American soldiers were standing guard and wouldn't let anyone in. My father and his friends hadn't come that far just to be turned away. They sat at the border, watching for the time when the soldiers changed posts, because they knew the border would probably be unsupervised, giving them the opportunity to cross. Through hours of observation, they learned that there was a five to eight minute gap when no one was patrolling the border. After an interminable wait, they finally saw their chance. The moment they saw that the guards' shift was over, and the replacements hadn't arrived yet, they ran across the border without detection.

The first town they came to was Schwandorf, where German refugees who had fled during the war were staying. Next, they traveled to Regensburg and were relieved to find that a Jewish committee, which took care of both Jews and non-Jews, had been established there. Having been starved for so long in the concentration camps and then having little to eat while traveling across borders, my father was relieved to find out that the Americans had supplied the town with plenty of food. The Jewish committee told my father that he could stay and even offered him a house that had belonged to a German family, but he refused because he wanted to look for my mother at Bergen-Belsen.

On his quest to find my mother, my father left Regensburg on a coal wagon and traveled three days and nights over five hundred miles. He arrived at Celle, eleven miles south of Bergen-Belsen. By that time, my parents knew the other had survived. My mother had gone to Mielec in Poland to find my father, and he had come to Bergen-Belsen to find her. They had missed each other. He decided to stay where he was and wait for her to come back. Finally, after three weeks, they were finally reunited.

After their reunion, they decided to stay in Bergen-Belsen, which had been converted into a displaced persons camp. There, they began to rebuild their lives and make sense of the magnitude of what they had experienced.

My parents were thrilled to learn of my mother's pregnancy and my birth in 1947.

Later in his life, my father told me that he was happy that he had come to the United States. He was proud to be an American. His grandson Sean and I were everything to him. Health and happiness were the most important things.

He was concerned that the survivors were getting older and would soon be gone. He said, "I would like somebody to carry the history of what happened to us during the Holocaust. The world, not just Jewish people. Everyone should know that six million people died for no reason. I lost my whole family. I had nobody. My wife lost her whole family." He hopes that his grandson Sean, the younger generation, will carry the story. "It shouldn't happen to anyone."

Concentration Camps where my father was imprisoned during the Holocaust:

- Ohrdruf (Germany)
- Bolkenhain (Germany)
- Buchenwald (Germany)
- Hirschberg (Germany)
- Gross Rosen (Germany)
- Stalowa Wola (Poland)
- Krakau-Plaszow (Poland)
- Mittelbau-Dora (Germany)
- Auschwitz III-Monowitz (Poland)

# Chapter 3
## The Chance to Bear Witness

$\mathcal{M}$y parents had both experienced Josef Schwammberger's cruelty and sadism. He had served in the forced labor camps where they had been imprisoned: as an SS officer in Przemysl and as the commandant of Mielec. He had ordered many killings, and he, himself, had killed as well as performed other sadistic acts.

After the war, Simon Wiesenthal, a survivor of five Nazi concentration camps, dedicated the rest of his life to search for and legally prosecute Nazi war criminals. Wiesenthal helped the U.S. intelligence agencies by gathering evidence in preparation for the trials of these criminals. He had drawn up a list of ten Nazi war criminals who were considered the most wanted. Josef Schwammberger was number five.

When my parents learned of Schwammberger's arrest in Argentina and his extradition to Germany in 1990, they were thrilled that he had been caught and hoped that he would be brought to justice. German prosecutor Kurt Schrimm traveled to many cities where survivors lived, gathering testimony for the trial. Both of my parents testified when the German court, consisting of Prosecutor Schrimm, Schwammberger's defense lawyer, and the judge, came to New York.

My mother described Schwammberger to me as a "rough, tough, bitter man, a very angry man." She recalled that he wore white gloves. He used to spin his gun around in his hand and then kill people. "He was a Jew hater." He was responsible for ordering the death of my three-year-old brother Emusch. Becoming obviously agitated, my mother described how difficult it was for her to give her testimony as evidence to Schwammberger's attorney. She knew that she might not remember every detail because fifty years had passed since she was in the camps. When asked specific questions that she couldn't answer, such as what kind of gloves Schwammberger wore, wool or cotton, or what his uniform looked like, my mother became infuriated. "I was afraid to look at him," she explained. My bold mother told the attorney, "If I would be you, I would be ashamed to defend him!"

My father was more successful in giving testimony. For six hours, he provided specific details of Schwammberger's killings and sadistic acts of torture. However, when my parents were given the opportunity to go to Germany to testify at Schwammberger's trial, they realized that they couldn't bear to be in the same room with him; they didn't want to look at him, to face him. Seeing him would bring them too much pain given all that they had been through. My parents had done as much as they were capable of. In addition, my father felt strongly that Schwammberger would never be adequately punished for the heinous crimes he committed, for all the people he killed. For so many years, Schwammberger had lived as a free man, and now at the age of seventy-eight, he would still have his life since there was no death penalty in Germany.

Originally charged with personally murdering or ordering the murder of over three thousand people, Schwammberger's charges had to be reduced to thirty-four because the prosecutors didn't have enough evidence. In 1992, Schwammberger was found guilty of seven counts of murder and thirty-two cases of accessory to murder and sentenced to life imprisonment. Schwammberger died in prison in 2004 at the age of ninety-two.

# Part 2

## My Story

Even now, after all these years have passed since my childhood, my anxiety still overwhelms me. My throat will close up, my heart will start to beat rapidly, and my stomach will begin to churn. My turmoil is visible in my eyes.

With all my life experiences, with all the love I have received, with all the tools I've been given, with all the logic and knowledge, I can, in an instant, become anxious. Although I have experienced joy and gratitude, those emotions do not preclude or prevent the feeling that everything is at risk, that life or the people I love can suddenly be pulled away from me. I am painfully of the belief that my son, grandchildren, or anyone I love can be gone in an instant. I never take their presence for granted.

I was raised to believe that if you were late, you were probably dead. If you were sick, you were dying. Since invariably someone I love would be unavoidably late or get sick, I was always living in a sense of loss, about to lose everything or everyone in a second. I constantly felt that I was in a hallway waiting, not knowing the outcome if I did not hear from a loved one who was supposed to call or was late. The waiting was unbearable. These feelings were instilled in me from an early age and have remained with me throughout my adult years.

Some demons can never be erased. I am the daughter of Holocaust survivors.

# Chapter 4

## The Smell of Dead People

*I* have few memories of my life as a young child living in the Bergen-Belsen Displaced Persons Camp. If you were to ask me what I remember most, it would have to be the smell that lingered over the camp, ever present. I doubt that I would have been able to identify the odor without hearing people refer to it as the smell of dead people. I did not understand the enormity of what had happened to cause the odor, but I sensed that something horrifying had happened. Once I formed that memory, I could conjure it up at will. It still haunts me today.

I was born on April 7, 1947. My parents named me Aviva, from the Hebrew word *aviv*, meaning spring, to commemorate the liberation of the camps in April of 1945. They were overjoyed with my birth. Out of the dark years of suffering and despair came a child, a symbol of their love and the beginning of their new life as a family. Years later, when I asked my mother why my birth certificate had the letters DP written on it, she told me it meant "Delightful Princess."

After the liberation, many concentration camps were opened and used as living quarters to house all of the survivors. My parents had nowhere else to go, having lost their homes and families. They had no choice but to begin their new life in the same place where they had been imprisoned and tortured.

Life became normal in abnormal circumstances. The survivors were still living behind barbed wire fences separated from the rest of the world. Some were in poor health. Living conditions, improved in comparison to the overcrowded, unsanitary, vermin-infested housing in the camps, were not optimum. However, in their attempt to begin life again, the survivors developed friendships, had children, and formed bonds; friends became family.

Since I had no knowledge of the harsh living conditions that my parents and the others had endured in the camps during the war, I felt safe in the familiar surroundings of the DP camp. I remember very little about this time in my young life, things like riding tricycles with a little boy named Jackie, a window slamming down on my fingers, being pushed off my tricycle. Yet, I know that I was not a carefree, whimsical child. I was an angry child who bit other children and fought with them.

The trauma for the survivors did not end after they were liberated. Most of them had no homes to return to, no communities, no institutions, no families. They had lost everything, even their health. All aspects of their former lives had been destroyed. While the long-term effects were not known at the time, they carried emotional and psychological wounds as well as physical problems.

Living with my parents and being among other survivors had a strong impact on me though I did not realize or understand it at the time. The other children and I constantly heard our parents exchange horror stories about their experiences in the various ghettos and camps. I internalized their dread and terror from the stories they told. My parents, especially my mother, who was deeply damaged from her losses and harsh treatment, passed on to me her anxiety and her fears.

I suspect that hearing the survivors talking about death, loss, torture, and distrust had a significant effect on my inability to eat solid food. Neither my parents nor I understood why I had this problem at the time. Whenever my mother tried to feed me, my throat would close up out of fear, and I could not swallow. I brought up food when I was forced to eat; the only way my mother could get me to eat anything at all was by straining the food. I remember hearing her say, "Esse, esse." My parents tried to approach eating as a fun activity, but nothing worked. I remember bananas more than any other food my mother tried to feed me. She mashed the bananas and combined them with sour cream or some other version of cream so that I would get some nutrition from the fruit and dairy. She wanted me to appear plump and healthy. Every time I saw her preparing the bananas and cream, I felt as if I was going to be subjected to some form of torture. As a result, my aversion to bananas lasted for most of my life. My refusal to eat was unimaginable to them, having been starved as prisoners in the concentration camps for so many years. They remembered scrounging for food, having someone give them a raw potato, meager rations of a bowl of watery soup, a piece of bread, never enough to sustain them.

Another fear I developed was of doctors wearing white, in fact, of anyone in a white uniform. Although I don't recall the original incident, I know something occurred during a time when my mother took me to see a doctor who terrorized me. As a result, whenever I saw a man in white, I would gag or throw up from fear. I still have an intense fear of doctors today.

These early signs of anxiety and fear, my inability to eat, and my fear of doctors in white coats became the driving forces in the development of my personality.

# Chapter 5

## Abandonment

$\mathcal{M}$y parents dreamed about leaving the Bergen-Belsen DP camp, but they knew they couldn't return to their hometowns because their homes, families, and friends were gone. Many survivors wanted to go to Israel, as did my parents. In fact, they had prepared to go, but my mother's sister Bela and her husband, who lived in Haifa, discouraged them, explaining that the economy was weak and that my parents would have difficulty finding work to support themselves financially. My parents were disappointed, especially my father, because he had dreamed of going to Israel before the war and had been active in a Zionist movement youth group, which entitled him to go.

With Israel no longer a possibility, and with my father having had surgery for a slipped disk and recovering in a convalescent home, my parents had to put off relocating. We seemed to be in a holding pattern, waiting to get out of Europe. The United States was finally opening its doors to Holocaust survivors with the Displaced Persons Act in 1948, but it limited the number of Jewish displaced persons who could come. In 1950, that Act was amended to remove those limits that had discriminated against them.

With the amendment of the Displaced Persons Act, my parents decided to emigrate to the United States. My father's cousin David Susskind and his family, who lived on Long Island, wanted us to come to New York. David wrote my parents that he had found a job for my father at an engraving company, so the decision was made. David sent us money for the journey.

When the decision was finally made to resettle in the United States, my parents often talked about what life would be like in a country they knew little about. Fortunately, the Susskind brothers and their families made all of the arrangements. We were lucky to have them care so much about our lives and our resettlement and to take such unselfish actions on our behalf. Although leaving Bergen-Belsen was bittersweet, being able to leave the memories was another story.

On July 2, 1950, my parents and I left Germany from the port city of Bremerhaven. We embarked on the USS General S. D. Sturgis, a World War II United States Navy military ship that was being used to transport displaced persons to the United States. As a three-year-old, I had always been with my parents and had never traveled outside of the DP camp. I did not know what to expect as a passenger on a large boat crowded with people for a six-week voyage. I soon learned that seasickness would be a constant companion for both my mother and me. Our quarters were in the lower deck, but we spent much of the time on the upper deck to get fresh air, relief from the malodorous odors from unwashed bodies and seasickness. My father had his hands full with us, trying to keep our hopes up, promising us that we would feel better and that the trip would soon be over. After that experience, my mother never stepped foot on a boat.

Coping with seasickness was certainly challenging, but getting lost on the boat introduced another significant trauma in my young life. Somehow, I became separated from my parents. They frantically looked everywhere, but they could not find me. Other adults on the boat who found me, a little girl alone and desperate to find her parents, tried to locate them among the swarm of passengers. As a young child, I had no notion of how much time had passed; I felt that I would never see my parents again, that I was alone in a sea of people I did not know. After what seemed like hours, I was finally reunited with my parents, but this traumatic experience had become internalized as a fear of loss and abandonment, which has stayed with me throughout my life.

Arriving at Ellis Island one early July morning remains another a strong memory for me. I was scared because I did not know what my life would be like in New York, but my parents were happy to start this new chapter. We had become part of history.

After such a long voyage, we were eager to see our relatives who had promised to come for us. We waited an entire day at the New York port only to realize that neither my father's uncle nor my mother's cousin was coming. We were stranded, abandoned.

Finally, to our relief, a representative from the Hebrew Immigrant Aid Society (HIAS), an organization that helps refugees, offered to assist us by providing dinner at the HIAS building. She told my father about an inexpensive hotel where we could stay. While this windowless hotel room with one bed was small, it was an improvement over the crowded boat and our seasickness. Our life in the United States had begun.

# Chapter 6

## Be Afraid, Don't Believe, Don't Trust

*L*iving in the tiny, one-bed, windowless hotel room provided by HIAS was better than coping with a lack of privacy and seasickness on the boat, but my father soon became suspicious about our lodgings when he noticed that men and women frequently entered a room in the hotel and left shortly after, not staying overnight. He did not want us living in a "whore house," as he referred to it, and wanted to get us out of there. After we had been living there for about a week, fortunately, my father's cousin, who had sent us money to come to the United States, visited us. My father told him that he didn't want any money; he just wanted to get the family out of that hotel as soon as possible. His cousin secured a job for my father in the shipping department of a company that made engraving machines. Finally, my father would be able to work and make an income so that we could afford a better place to live.

Through a connection my father made with a woman he met at the HIAS building, where survivors frequently congregated, he learned of a small apartment she had for rent in Brownsville, Brooklyn. The two of them took the subway to look at it, and my father was, in his words, "the happiest guy" when he saw it. The apartment was freshly painted and had a little refrigerator. When he asked the woman about the cost of rent, she told him $36 a month, but she insisted, "You have to put under the table $400." My father made a deal, paying her $200 that day. He did not tell my mother about it right away because he wanted to surprise her by getting it ready for us with furniture, food, and other necessities. He carried out his plan by telling my

45

mother that they were going to look at an apartment, not that he had already rented it. After showing her the apartment, beaming with pride about the refrigerator he had stocked with food, he asked if she liked it. When she told him she did, my father proudly exclaimed, "This is yours." My mother could hardly believe it. We moved in eight days later.

Our apartment was located above a laundromat on Riverdale Avenue. In the front of the building, two doors were positioned side by side, one to enter our apartment, the other to enter the laundromat. A stairway led to our rooms: a large room which served as a kitchen/living area and an alcove with two beds, one for my parents and the other for me. The living area was multipurpose, equipped with a stove, sink, icebox, and sofa. I was surprised when I saw that the apartment did not have a separate bathroom with a sink, tub, and toilet. Instead, the bathtub was in the living area, while the toilet was in a separate small room with a door. We had to bathe in the open area, which made me uncomfortable because I felt exposed. What I remember most about this apartment was the persistent problem of water bugs and roaches. To this day I am phobic about bugs.

After we were settled in our apartment, my father started his new job, working in a shipping department. The job required that he lift heavy objects, which was difficult for him because of his back problems, but he couldn't tell his boss that he had a bad back because he needed the job to support our family. After two years, he was promoted to the position of manager of the shipping department, satisfied that he had a good job and enough money to support the family.

My mother was a homemaker, so during my formative years, we spent a great deal of time together. She was my role model, my teacher, and I learned and copied her behaviors and attitudes. The trauma of the Holocaust was alive within her, dominating her thoughts and behavior. All that she had witnessed and experienced, all her losses, became infused in her world view. She always feared the worst and told me to expect it. I never felt angry or resentful of my mother because I must have known on some level that she wished she could have behaved differently or that she had the choice to be any other way. An incredibly worried and anxious woman, my mother didn't know how to keep her fears from me or hide her anxiety, so I inhaled hers. Whatever she felt, I felt. The message was always be afraid, don't believe, don't trust, and always make sure that I see her.

For example, I understood the concept of my father leaving the house every day to go to work and coming home at dinner time. But I soon learned one of her major fears, that my father would not return from work at the end of the day. An hour before it was time for him to arrive home, my mother became anxious, constantly looking at the clock. I watched as she paced the floor, repeatedly looked out the window, slapped her forehead, and cried. Would this be the day that he would not return?

My anxiety manifested in my inability to eat, which continued to be a problem and a source of worry and frustration for my parents, who did not know how to help me. Food and mealtimes were extremely anxiety producing and torturous. I was always frightened and could not swallow; I gagged when trying to chew solid food. Worried that I was not getting any nourishment, my parents came up with the idea to buy a food grinder so that I could swallow the food my mother cooked without my having to chew. While grinding the food helped to some extent, I always threw up part of the meal. While I was asking myself why they were forcing me to eat, they were saying, "How could you do this to us?"

When I was old enough to go to kindergarten, my anxiety over knowing my mother would leave me was so overwhelming that I refused to let her go. I would throw a tantrum, hold my breath, or vomit. The thought of not being able to visibly see where my mother was at all times was torturous. She kept trying to soothe me, promising me that everything would be okay. She said, "Look at the other children. See how good they are?" But I was inconsolable. In an effort to help me, the principal allowed my mother to sit on a little stool next to me so that I would calm down and get used to being in the classroom. Having my mother with me, unfortunately, did not make a difference, and I did not finish out that year in kindergarten.

With the negative experience in kindergarten behind me, I began to feel more comfortable in school. However, although I was present physically, I had difficulty retaining my lessons. I spent much of the day worrying about whether my mother would be there to meet me after school, worried that she might not come, that something happened to her. If I didn't see her immediately after the bell rang, I panicked.

Another worry for me was my obsessive need to know where my parents were at all times. In fact, I always slept on the floor next to my parents' bed. Even though I had an area for my own bed, I had assigned myself without realizing it to be my parents' guardian. I felt responsible for their well-being at all times. The only way I could protect them at night when I couldn't see them was to sleep next to them. I had to watch them, and I remember many occasions when I did not sleep through the night. My purposeful watchfulness eased my anxiety about my parents' welfare during the night, but on occasion, I was disturbed by the noises they were making during their intimate activities. My parents probably thought that I was sleeping, but I was always on high alert, sensitive to every sound and movement. I didn't know what they were doing, but I felt uncomfortable and nauseated. I wanted them to stop and covered my ears. I was young and impressionable, not knowing anything about sexual intimacy, so I drew my own conclusions from my mother's reactions. She did not seem to be an active participant and grudgingly submitted to my father's advances, leading me to believe that she wasn't deriving pleasure. I didn't want my parents to know that I had been awake during their intimate moments, so I never asked them about it, leaving me with a distorted interpretation that continued throughout my childhood.

One incident in particular remains an indelible memory of this fear of being left alone without them. When the weather was pleasant, my parents liked to sit on wooden crates outside our apartment after dinner. They enjoyed interacting with neighbors, particularly my mother, who was the social one. Sometimes I joined them when I did not have school the next day. On other nights, after I finished my homework, I had to go to bed. One night, I woke up and immediately ran to the window that looked out onto the street to check on my parents. I did not see them or hear their or anyone else's voices, which threw me into a panic. I did not know that they were sitting close to the building, so they were not visible from the window because of a small overhang. Hoping that they would hear me, I repeatedly banged on the window to attract their attention to no avail. My frantic pounding broke the window, cutting my hand. Hearing the glass break, my parents ran up to the apartment. They, too, became hysterical when they saw me crying, with cuts on my hands and broken glass everywhere. After cleaning my cuts, swabbing them with mercurochrome, and bandaging my hands, I calmed down. This incident alerted my parents to the extent of my desperate need to be with them.

The need to protect my parents gradually extended to looking out for potential dangers they might encounter when walking outside. Every Friday night, after observing Shabbos by sharing a challah, lighting the candles, and blessing the wine, my parents and I walked to an orthodox synagogue. I was too young to be left alone in the house, so I accompanied them. I did not mind going because at least I could see them. I recall that I always walked in front of them because I wanted to protect them from a crack or hole in the sidewalk that might cause them to fall and hurt themselves.

As if trauma at school and anxiety at home weren't enough, I experienced a distressing event after which I refused to speak in public. Having been born in Germany, German was the language I spoke for the first three years of my life. When I was around four or five, my mother and I were shopping in a local grocery store not far from our home in Brooklyn. I had not learned English yet, so in German, I asked my mother for something I wanted. When the store owner heard us talking, he thought we were Nazis, not German Jews or Jews born in Germany who were Polish. He did not know that my mother was a Holocaust survivor. In his rush to judgment, he grabbed a broom and screaming at us, chased us out of the store. My mother broke down in tears and could hardly speak. She said in Yiddish, "He knows not what he is doing to us." This terrifying incident affected me greatly. As a result, I refused to speak outside the house for a year. People thought I was unable to talk.

I had become a frightened, anxious child.

# Chapter 7

## Keeping Secrets

$\mathcal{M}$y mother's words, "don't tell, be afraid, and don't trust," were ingrained in me for so long that they had become a part of my belief system, affecting my thoughts, actions, and interactions with others. I was not a worry-free, carefree child. All I ever wanted was to be like everyone else, but I felt that everything about me was different.

I didn't realize how different I was from other children until I started spending time with little girls my age. I saw how happy they were, laughing freely and having fun, whether at a party or playing with dolls. I had no real understanding of the joy they were experiencing. Because I didn't know what they were smiling about, I copied their facial expressions, but my smile wasn't genuine. I was so nervous when I was with them that I couldn't enjoy myself, but I did my best to look like the part. Adding to my discomfort was my ever present worry that I wasn't at home to watch my parents. On the other hand, I really didn't want to go home to watch them.

I realized that there was something dreadfully wrong in the way I interpreted and experienced events compared to the way my friends did. I labeled my differences as defects, and I didn't want them to know how defective I was. I was ashamed that I was different and terrified that if my friends found out what I was really like, they wouldn't want to play with me, so I had to protect the way I was feeling. My parents had taught me not to let anyone know my real thoughts or secrets because doing so would hurt me.

Not only was I uncomfortable interacting with my friends, but also, I was embarrassed because my appearance was different. My mother sewed my clothes, and while they were beautifully executed, they just didn't look like everyone else's. Even if the clothes were similar to those of the other girls, they looked different because of the way my mother styled them. She dressed me as if I still lived in Poland or Germany. I was the only girl at school wearing suspenders with a white cotton shirt that buttoned down the front. My hairstyle was also different from the other girls. Unlike the single braid the other girls wore, my hair was braided in two pigtails as was the style in Europe. I always had to wear undershirts because she didn't want me to "catch a chill," even in warm weather. The undershirt requirement continued even when I started wearing a bra; I had to wear it over the bra so no one would see it. I was mortified.

Another one of my secrets was that although I loved my parents very much, I was secretly ashamed of them. My mother wasn't like my friends' mothers. She looked European, spoke with an accent, and was much older. When I went to other children's homes, I saw how different their lives were from mine. Their parents were much younger, they didn't have accents, and they didn't have numbers tattooed on their arms. So I told my friends that my parents were really my grandparents.

The secret I carried for many years that contributed to my deep sense of shame was being repeatedly groped by a neighbor. At that time of the abuse, I was between the ages of eleven and twelve. We lived on a street where all of our neighbors were Holocaust survivors. My mother developed a close friendship with one of the women, and I was often given the task of going to her house to give something to her or get something from her. When she wasn't looking, her husband took advantage of my innocence by pressing me close to him, trying to stick his tongue in my mouth, and putting his hands on my buttocks. I could feel his erection, but I felt powerless, unable to do anything to stop him. I was embarrassed and ashamed, but I was not comfortable telling my parents about what he had done, knowing that he and his wife were Holocaust survivors like my parents. I could neither add to his troubled life nor hurt my mother's friend. My mother would have been devastated to learn about what had happened, and she would have ended their friendship. If my father had found out, I can tell you that the situation would not have ended well.

My neighbor's abuse had long term effects on me. It took me quite some time to recover because I had no one whom I could talk to about what had happened, no one to confront him and make him stop, and no one to help me process my feelings. I transferred my mistrust of men to my father; I shied away from opportunities to be close to him. I was disgusted and ashamed every time I thought about what my neighbor did to me. I felt that I was defective, that I was broken, that something was wrong with me to allow someone to exploit me that way for his own gratification. I wondered what it was about me that would make someone think it was okay to take advantage of a child in that way.

Over time, my need to protect my secrets caused me to become the person other people wanted to see, not the person I really was. I would not let them see that I was disturbed. I knew how to cover it up very well. The more secrets I had, the more I protected them, and the more they owned me. Nobody knew how terribly broken and troubled I was. I wanted to disappear.

Pastor Rick Warren, in one of his teachings, wrote, "You're only as sick as your secrets." I didn't know or understand this concept as a child, but holding on to my secrets became a pattern that kept me sick for a long time.

# Chapter 8

## Bearing Witness

*I* grew up hearing the stories of my parents' experiences during the Holocaust. When I was much younger, my parents, who the Germans had sent to different camps during the war, talked to each other about what they went through. I sensed that something bad had happened to them, hearing them refer with contempt to Hitler, and I saw how upset they became. In some ways my parents would tell me too much about death and loss. At other times, they would be secretive. When they didn't want me to hear, they spoke in Polish or in Yiddish warning, "Don't let Aviva hear," or "Don't tell Aviva." My parents thought I didn't understand what they were saying, but I had begun to learn those languages and could understand some of their conversations.

When I was nine years old, we moved to Forest Hills, and my exposure to more stories of what happened to people during the Holocaust increased. Due to an increase in crime in Brooklyn, my father became concerned about our safety, so he decided to move us out. An immigrant working long factory hours, my father had saved enough money to buy a two-family house in Forest Hills on Selfridge Street. He found a tenant, whose rent payments helped him pay down the mortgage quickly.

I had never seen a community like Forest Hills. I was used to our small apartment, the city streets, traffic, and noise. Although our new home was a two-family structure in a modest part of Forest Hills, I was thrilled to be out of our tiny, bug-infested apartment. For the first time, I had my own separate bedroom. To my delight, we had a separate bathroom: no more tub in the kitchen.

Soon after we moved in, my parents learned that Holocaust survivors lived in every two-family house for two blocks. None of them knew each other from the concentration camps or the DP camps, but they quickly grew close and thought of each other as sisters and brothers. They developed a deep bond as did I.

This tightly knit group frequently entertained each other in their homes. I remember when everyone came to our home. They played cards, drank coffee with a lump of sugar under their tongue, and talked, most often reminiscing about what had happened to them during the Holocaust. They told the same stories over and over, recounting beatings, hard labor, extreme heat or cold, lack of privacy, uncleanliness, and marches.

When I first heard their stories, I felt sorry. I did not truly understand the pain and sorrow of their suffering. I just knew that when they talked about it, I was deeply affected, that familiar knot in my stomach increasing . I didn't want to hear about their experiences, yet at the same time I felt disloyal if I didn't listen, that I would be disrespectful to tell them to stop speaking of it.

All the talk about death and loss permeated me. I was sure that something would happen to my parents, that they would die. I felt that I needed to protect them because of what they had gone through. It was my job on earth to provide them with happiness at all times, to cause them no pain, and to understand. I did not want to do anything to make them sad or worried. In my need to make sure I protected my parents at all times, I continued sleeping on the floor of their bedroom next to my mother's side of the bed as I had done in our first apartment. When we walked to synagogue on Friday nights and on other holidays, I walked in front of my them to watch for cracks or holes in the streets to prevent them from falling.

As I got older, I acquired a deeper level of understanding, and all of the heartbreaking stories I heard from my parents and their friends began to affect me more profoundly. I found it unbearable to hear the stories over and over. At times, I grew numb to them, their talk becoming background noise. On other occasions, I would go to my room and put a pillow over my head to muffle their conversations. Soon my feelings quickly turned into terrible rage. I wanted to go to Poland and Germany to find Nazis and kill them.

The weight of knowing what my parents suffered and my inability to have anyone help me process my feelings drove me to many negative behaviors at an early age. I tried to be a "good" child, one who was polite, caring and respectful, but I could not maintain this persona all the time. I did not realize that I felt resentful or angry. I felt torn between trying to please them and hating what they were asking of me. I was caught in the middle of being obedient and respectful and of being rebellious. When I was disrespectful, I felt terribly guilty. I was constantly playing ping pong with myself.

I developed a pattern of being contrary and lying. If you asked me if was raining, and I knew it was sunny outside, I would say that it was raining. Still experiencing anxiety that affected my ability to eat, at dinner time, I used to hide food in my underwear when my parents were not looking and throw the uneaten portions out later. At other times, I would lie and tell them that I had eaten something in school. This pattern of lying would continue through adulthood.

Another negative behavior manifested when, for a short time, I became a kleptomaniac. I used to go to Woolworth's, the famous discount department store, and steal small, inconsequential items like doll clothing. I did not understand why I had felt that I had to steal these items, but doing so made me feel powerful. I experienced a feeling of exhilaration, which changed my mood and numbed my feelings. After I brought those stolen items home, I had no use for them. No one knew what I had done, and my parents would have been mortified if they found out because they were very honest people. I remember times when my father found money in the street, and instead of keeping it, he would try to find the person who lost it.

Although I did not know it then, my behaviors were coping strategies. No one knew how sad I was, how terrified I was of many things, because on the outside, I did all I could to look and act as if everything in my life was normal. Yet in reality, I felt that I had a lot of secret compartments and secret lives. I felt a high level of dread, wanting to run from myself, which intensified over time, leading me to find other ways to numb my tangled emotions.

# Chapter 9

## Surveillance

My parents, especially my mother, thought the moon, the sun, and the stars rose with me. But because my parents had lost their families and my baby brother during the Holocaust, they felt the need to protect me relentlessly. When I was a child, I was not aware that they were being overprotective, but I began to realize this as I got older. While I understood their reasons, their constant protection, worry, and fear, their trying to rope me off from everything, made me resentful.

The talk at home was always filled with worry about me. I was their primary focus. If I didn't look happy, if my eyes didn't shine, if my voice sounded tired, my demeanor became the focus of my parents' discussion and questioning. I felt like I was being grilled. "Something is wrong. Tell me what's wrong." Every day, I endured their constant worrying and questioning.

During my first few years in elementary school, I didn't make any friends because my focus was on watching the clock for the end of the day when I would see my mother. She was so worried about my lack of friends that without my agreement, she decided to take matters into her own hands. She selected children from in my class, whom she saw when she came to pick me up, and invited those she thought would be appropriate to our home. Her efforts were unsuccessful though because I wasn't capable of developing friendships at that time in my life due to my anxiety.

Restrictions and parental control became a part of my everyday life. When I was eleven, if I wanted to go to a girlfriend's house, I was not allowed to cross the streets without my parents' supervision. They also controlled what I watched on television. I wasn't allowed to watch a popular show, *77 Sunset Strip*, because it had the word *strip* in it. They never watched the show, so they didn't know that the series was about private detectives.

As I got older, my parents' need to know what I was doing at all times evolved into their practice of following me. When I went to a friend's house three blocks away, my mother had to follow me by foot and see exactly where the house was. On other occasions, my father followed me in his car. For instance, before I started dating, my male and female friends and I often met at the neighborhood ice cream parlor or candy store to socialize. My mother insisted that my father follow me in his turquoise Ford Fairlane. I knew if I turned around, I'd see the car. Wherever I went, day or night, I knew to expect to see his car circling the block. My friends noticed too, and, of course, I was embarrassed and humiliated. The surveillance continued when I was old enough to date and when my parents allowed it. The boys I knew didn't have cars, so we traveled to our destination by bus. I knew my parents were following us in the Ford. In my teens, if a boy I was dating had a car, my father wrote down the license plate of the boy's car in front of him.

Their continued focus on me wasn't limited to my activities away from home. I had absolutely no privacy when I was at home. They read my mail and listened to my phone calls. Every aspect of my life was monitored. I felt caged. As a result, I kept secrets, I snuck, I lied. I lied about homework, test grades, the food I ate, and the people I saw. If my lips were moving, I was lying.

# Chapter 10

## Numbing the Fear

My first taste of an alcoholic beverage was a sip of the sweet and fruity Slivovitz plum brandy, popular in Central and Eastern Europe, that my father used to enjoy. Every night when he came home from a long day of work, he would pour one shot of brandy into a little glass, drink it, and then put the bottle away. I was a child and didn't yet realize how alcohol would change my life.

I made the decision to drink illegally when I was thirteen. I attended a party at a friend's home, and someone brought liquor that he had stolen from a parent's cabinet. I didn't like the way it tasted, but I didn't care because I loved the way the alcohol made me feel; it lifted my anxiety. I immediately made friends with the freedom that drinking alcohol gave me: no more anxiety, no more fear. I felt whole.

During those early teen years, my drinking was dependent on finding opportunities to secretly consume alcohol when I visited friends' homes. All of my friends' parents had a cabinet of some sort in which they kept their liquor. Upon entering a friend's home, I scanned the various rooms where I thought the alcohol was kept, made a mental note of its location, and planned my strategy to sneak a drink so that no one would see me or know what I was doing. During the visit with my friend, I would tell her that I needed to use the bathroom. Then I would take a detour to the room where the liquor was, grab a bottle, and chug as much of it as I could until I gagged. Once I knew the drill, I could do it in half the time. I don't know if my friends suspected that I had been drinking, but when I returned from the bathroom, they knew something was different about me though they didn't speak of it.

My mother, however, did notice something different about me that she couldn't identify. I recall a number of times when she asked if I was okay because I was behaving strangely. Actually, I was under the influence, so my behavior was different. Off we went to the medical doctor because she knew something was not quite right, but she didn't know exactly what it was. My mother was always dragging me to the doctor for something. If I had a cough for more than one day, she immediately thought it was tuberculosis. According to my mother, if I was coughing, I was dying. This particular appointment was with a psychiatrist. My mother mentioned that she thought that I had been drinking. The doctor asked me very personal questions, and my answers revealed to him that I was deeply troubled. The doctor told my mother, "Mrs. Susskind, I don't know if you know, but your daughter has started drinking. It was a good thing because if she hadn't, she would have killed herself because she was carrying so much." He told her that the sorrow and pain I felt because of what my parents went through was insurmountable.

I wasn't drinking on a regular basis given my age and few opportunities to do so. But something else was changing within me. I started to separate from myself. I didn't want to be in my reality, so I formed a different one. I even gave myself a different name. I became Vivian. When I could, I thought of myself as Vivian. She was a normal person, while I was not. As Vivian, I was more confident when speaking to anyone in school who didn't know much about me. I felt comfortable in my own skin. This phase didn't last long but clearly was an indication that I would find other ways to attempt to escape the anxiety and fear.

More troubling was that there were times when I couldn't remember parts of my day or evening. I thought I was a little insane, not knowing or having anyone to talk to about it. I actually thought those blackouts were the beginning of insanity.

# Chapter 11

## The Joy of Eating

After many years of feeling agitated at the prospect of eating, and gagging at the smell and sight of food, I finally turned a corner at age thirteen. Usually, I refused dinner invitations because eating was such a horror for me, like having a tooth pulled. But when my friend invited me to have dinner at her house, I agreed. The family ordered a combination of corned beef and pastrami sandwiches on rye bread with Russian dressing and coleslaw from the Turnpike Deli in Forest Hills, Queens. As I watched my friend and her family eat the sandwiches, I tried to figure out how my mother could strain the sandwich so that I could enjoy the taste without having to chew it. My friend said, "Take a bite! Doesn't it smell good?" I smelled it, took a bite, and, like magic, I loved it. My friends and parents celebrated, and this event became the Turnpike Deli story. After that, I began to eat normally. I began to love food.

Once I made the transition from swallowing strained food to actually chewing my food and enjoying it, anxiety continued to play a role in my eating habits. Between the ages of thirteen and sixteen, my weight went up and down. Sometimes I couldn't eat because of my anxiety, and other times I ate to soothe myself. I started to eat my feelings. Also, when I drank, I became hungrier.

As horrified as my mother was about my not eating, she was also upset at my sneaking and hiding food and eating late at night. Always excessively doting on and worried about me, my mother noticed that I had gained weight. Although my mother was never mean, she made a remark that was hurtful, "Aviva, you're wearing the same size as me. My clothes are looking tight on you." Others noticed my weight gain as well. When a boy in high school said to me, "You know, you would be so pretty if you weren't so fat," I was humiliated, embarrassed, and self-conscious. I hadn't seen myself as a fat person. After that, I started restricting food. I became obsessed with being thin. I took Dexatrim, which was sold over the counter, no doctor's prescription needed. It contained the drug PPA (phenylpropanolamine), an amphetamine-type substance. So in addition to restricting food, I added excessive exercise; a couple of times a week I took very long walks from one city to the next and then back home. From Queens to Manhattan over the 59th Street Bridge was around twenty-five miles. I soon lost all the weight I had gained, but I didn't stop taking Dexatrim to keep my weight down. This drug made me feel hyper; my heart felt like it was jumping out of my chest. So in order to calm down, I would sneak more drinks.

My nails, hair, and teeth were most affected by my eating problems. My hair became very thin, and by the time I was nineteen, I had to use hair pieces and wigs to create the illusion that I had a full head of hair. I also suffered from tooth loss on my upper jaw and had to have implants to replace them.

Restricting food or overeating, over-exercising, and drinking alcohol had become my coping mechanisms for my stress, anxiety, and fear. I later learned during my recovery that these behaviors often occur together, particularly in women. However, during my teen years, I was unaware of what I was doing to myself and had no one to help me.

# Chapter 12

## Crossing the Invisible Line

*D*uring my years in high school and college, alcohol had become a friend, helping me function emotionally, helping me escape being fearful and scared all the time. My nerves were so bad that I could not go too long without a sip, so I carried with me a large seltzer bottle spiked with lots of vodka.

When I finished high school, I decided that I wanted to go to college. I chose New York University even though I knew that paying the tuition would be difficult for my parents. I understood how hard my father worked, and I wasn't frivolous with their money ordinarily, but I insisted. Unfortunately, I found it difficult to concentrate on my classes though I didn't know why at the time. I realized that I was wasting my parents' money soon after I started. To save money, I transferred to Queens College, but my attendance there didn't last long. I began to understand that I didn't like school.

When I met Steve, I was no longer interested in moving forward with college. I was eighteen and had a job in the garment center. Our relationship quickly became serious. Several months after we started dating, and with my parents' permission, he spent the weekends at our house so Steve could avoid the expense of gas or tolls to return home. He slept in our finished basement, and I used to sneak downstairs to be with him. My parents loved Steve and thought he was a good match for me. He was a devoted son to his mother and showed respect for my parents, a quality they admired. They accepted him as part of the family and treated us to occasional dinners out on Saturday nights.

Steve didn't know about my drinking then. He just thought that I had mood swings and personality changes along with my constant worry. At that time, I didn't drink all day and night; I was just drinking enough to self-medicate, sneaking alcohol whenever I could only sips at a time, but it took the edge off.

I married Steve when I was twenty. I was happy to be out of my parents' home and under their watchful eyes, away from the constant memories and discomfort that I wanted to escape, which made me feel guilty for thinking these thoughts because I loved my parents.

We rented an apartment in Forest Hills, Queens, which, as a new bride, I was excited about furnishing. I wanted my new home to look and feel different from my parents' home, to reflect my personality and taste with glitz and drama. Together, Steve and I purchased dark, heavy Mediterranean furniture, in fashion at the time, which contrasted nicely with our white wall-to-wall carpeting. For a little eye appeal, I chose fuchsia club chairs. While we were setting up our apartment, I had something new to focus on and didn't need to drink as much.

My fresh start was short-lived. A few months after we moved in, I woke up in the middle of the night to find a roach crawling on me. In a flash, I was transported back to that roach and water bug infested apartment over a laundromat in Brooklyn where my parents and I lived when we first came to the United States. As a child living in that environment, I had developed a phobia of bugs. Terror consumed me; I couldn't stay in our new apartment another minute. I fled to a hotel that night. The next day, I gave Steve the task of fumigating all the furniture, while I took every article of clothing to the cleaners. We vacated the apartment as soon as we could and found another apartment in the same area. The incident triggered the fears that I had hoped to leave behind, and little by little, my drinking increased.

The first year of our marriage was a good year. I felt grateful that I had someone sleeping next to me. Steve was easy to talk to. I felt safe with him. I did drink alcohol, but it wasn't causing me any problems. I drank on a regular basis during the day but not enough for Steve to notice. Although I was happy to be married and on my own with my husband, I felt a sadness, a disappointment, but I couldn't identify what was causing it. I had thought Steve was my savior, that being married would change the anxiety and fear I had felt most of my life, but it didn't. So I started drinking more to help me cope. My behavior became frightening to Steve, and I was having difficulty hiding it. Alcohol was taking over my life. I no longer had control of the outcome of my drinking. I had crossed that invisible line.

My never-ending pattern of anxiety and worry for my parents now expanded to include Steve. I insisted that he check in with me when he was at work to let me know that he was safe. If he had any work-related travel on weekends, I had to go with him. When he was late coming home from work, I exhibited a similar pattern of distress that I had learned from my mother when she waited for my father. I recall one incident that was extremely stressful and illustrates the extent of my anxiety. Years before my son Sean was born, Steve had called to tell me he was on his way to my parents' house in Forest Hills, Queens from New York City. We used to have dinner at my parents' house once a week, so I was already there waiting for him to arrive. Steve told me to meet him on the corner of Queens Boulevard and Continental Avenue, an area with shopping and restaurants. He was supposed to be there around five o'clock. As I waited, gray clouds darkened the sky, a huge storm looming on the horizon. I called my mother and told her that Steve hadn't arrived yet. When she heard my voice filled with anxiety, she immediately panicked as well and automatically decided that we should worry together. She walked from her house to the designated corner and waited with me. Soon after, the storm moved in with a vengeance, raining heavily. Bolts of lightning lit up the sky around us, followed by thunder filling the air. Standing under the single umbrella that my mother had brought, we waited as the storm raged around us. Every time we saw the headlights of a car pulling in, we desperately searched for Steve as the windshield wipers briefly revealed the driver, but to no avail. Worry and anxiety were our companions as we stood in the rain for four hours, soaked through our clothing. Neither my mother nor I ever thought to go home or that Steve would come to the house if we weren't waiting on the corner for him. When Steve finally pulled up, he knew that because of my anxiety, I would be waiting for him in the rain. Wind, rain, darkness, nor cold could have kept me from waiting on that corner.

About two years after I was married to Steve, I drank so much that I passed out, and he couldn't wake me up. Overwhelmed with worry, he called 911 and my parents, who were distraught about hearing what had happened. I was transported to the hospital emergency room where Steve and my parents waited for the doctor to inform them about my condition. After the doctor had pumped my stomach, clearing the toxins from my body, he told my family that I had suffered from alcohol poisoning. If Steve hadn't been home, I would have died.

My drinking was no longer a secret. I attempted to make excuses, explaining that I only drank alcohol that one time. Of course, they knew otherwise. They realized that their confusion about my behavior was due to my alcohol intake. But I was in denial. I had no idea what tornado lay head.

# Chapter 13

## A New Home, A New Baby, A Divorce

After being married for a few years, Steve and I moved into a brand new housing development in Dix Hills. We had been advised not to buy this expensive, brand new home in the first place, but we were young, in our early twenties, and determined to live in that affluent neighborhood. The two-story house was large, with four bedrooms, and was on an acre of land. We would have been better off with a resale.

Despite the fact that we were house poor, we moved forward with our lives, both of us working full time. I had wanted to have a baby even though I wasn't whole enough within myself to take on the gift of being a parent. We tried to get pregnant for a long time. I was depressed that I hadn't conceived while my friends had. I feared that I would be childless and that I wasn't meant to have a child, but rather that I should devote more time to work because we needed extra money to support the house. I prayed in earnest, and when my prayers were finally answered, my dream came true. After I had gone to the gynecologist for a regular exam, he called and told me, "The rabbit died," an expression used in the past to tell a woman she was pregnant. Finally, at the age of twenty-two, I was elated. Now I would be happy, I thought.

I had been drinking regularly when I learned that I was two months pregnant, so I stopped immediately. My joy turned to fear when my pregnancy took an unexpected turn; Sean was born prematurely in my seventh month. Steve and I rushed to Beth Israel Hospital in Manhattan where I learned that Sean was in a breech position. The doctor tried to turn him to no avail. After twenty hours in labor, Sean entered the world through a forceps-assisted delivery. As a result, he had a hernia and a concave chest. He weighed only four pounds three ounces and was jaundiced, so he had to stay in the hospital for eight weeks. I was extremely upset that the doctor had allowed such a long labor and delivery. After Sean's delivery, I suffered from undiagnosed postpartum depression and thought I was crazy, so I started to drink again to cope with my emotional state. I never went for help about my feelings. When I was finally able to bring Sean home from the hospital, I realized that I didn't know much about caring for a child, but after my initial panic, we developed a strong bond. Sean was such a good baby with a great disposition.

My neighbors were all young with young children, all house poor. Because Steve and I had only one car, I drove him to the train station every day like all the other wives in our community did. After taking our husbands to the train station, the wives took turns bringing their babies to each other's homes. The first time they came to my house for coffee, as the hostess, I asked them, "What would you like in your coffee, vodka or scotch?" This seemed like an ordinary question to me until I noticed that they looked at each other in disbelief and then at me. Seeing their reaction, I immediately told them that I was joking. At that moment I realized that they lived their lives without alcohol. They seemed to manage their lives better than I did. I wondered how they did it. Weren't they anxious and worried all the time? How could they stand it if they didn't drink?

Sean was so easy to take care of that I found that I had extra time on my hands. Extra time with not much to do was dangerous for me because for an alcoholic, an idle mind leads to boredom, and I didn't like to be by myself with nothing to do. Although I didn't want to leave Sean to go back to my full-time job in the garment district, I needed something else to fill my time. I wanted to work and contribute financially to the household, but at that time, we didn't have the money to buy a business. I came up with the idea to start my own boutique, which gave me an opportunity to keep myself occupied and to help out with expenses. Steve and I bought a used school bus, and together we transformed the bus into a boutique on wheels. We pulled out all of the seats, put carpet on the floor, decorated the interior, and created an area with a curtain around it for Sean's playpen so that I could have him with me. I wanted to stimulate interest for this boutique in an unusual way, so Steve and I had three sets of flyers printed. The first one we distributed had two words: "The Bus." I wanted people to wonder what the bus was and why it was coming. A few weeks later, we circulated the second set of flyers, which announced, "Watch for the Bus." "The Bus Is Coming to You" was written on the last set. After getting a peddler's license and learning how to drive the bus, I was ready. I was not allowed to park the bus in any lot near malls or schools, so I had to drive from one community to another. Unfortunately, I began this venture in the winter, so people were not out and about, and if they hadn't seen all three flyers, they wouldn't know why a school bus, the outside of which we hadn't decorated, was pulling into their neighborhood. Unfortunately, the boutique didn't do as well as I had hoped, but it was a fun venture while it lasted. We sold the bus to a man who put it to good use as a camper for his family.

The financial loss from the failure of the boutique on wheels was compounded by a car fire that almost took our lives. Steve loved cars and had seen a used Lincoln Continental that he wanted to buy. The salesman tried to discourage him, but Steve wanted it. One day, Steve and I, with Sean in his seat in the back of the car, were driving to our home on the Long Island Expressway from my parents' home in Forest Hills when I saw sparks coming from the car. I mentioned this to Steve, but he didn't believe me. All of a sudden, the car was engulfed in flames. Steve jumped out of the car, quickly grabbing Sean out of his seat as I leapt out of the front passenger side. The three of us stood on the road and watched as the entire car exploded before our eyes. I learned how quickly life is about seconds and inches; one second and one inch can sometimes make all the difference. It would take me many years before I would truly understand what this meant.

I was deeply shaken by this incident, which added to my state of high anxiety. As well, I found myself once again with time on my hands. I was young and immature, a person with emotional issues who needed to self-medicate with alcohol to get through the day. As the years went by and my drinking escalated, the more I drank, the more I disappeared. Soon there was no Aviva to love. But I couldn't stop. I couldn't do it for Sean; I couldn't do it for Steve or my parents, and I loved them all so much. I was addicted. I didn't have the power of choice anymore. Love was not enough.

My marriage to Steve began to fall apart. When we met, I believed that he was the one who could make me happy. He doted on me, loved me, and understood me. When I succumbed to alcoholism, our relationship deteriorated. He had visions of a different life than the one he had. I remember him saying to me, "Aviva, I can't take this anymore." He warned me constantly about what he was going to do if I didn't get sober or change. He would say, "I'm miserable. I'm unhappy. I'm worried. You're using me up." I can understand how difficult it must have been to be living with someone who was erratic, dysfunctional, and depressed, leading him to stray. I didn't know then that no one could make me feel whole as a person, that happiness comes from within. If I hadn't been drinking, I could have been a better wife. My drinking distorted all his good qualities. While Steve was a good husband, he could have worked harder at being a parent.

In addition to dealing with our troubled marriage, my ever-present anxiety was exacerbated by the financial pressures of owning our home, which we could no longer afford. Our home went into foreclosure and was listed in the local papers; everyone knew about it. I was mortified and filled with shame, so I drank more to cope. We put our house up for sale and rented a house in Great Neck, eventually buying a home there after the sale of the Dix Hills house. Our home in Great Neck was located in an upscale community, but ours was more modest, not representative of the rest of the community. We moved there because I had purchased a small beauty franchise, offering manicures, pedicures, electrolysis, and facials, making it possible for me to work close to home and be near Sean rather than returning to my former job at the garment center in the city.

Finally, Steve could no longer deal with my drinking, and we separated. Sean was eight years old. A year later, Steve and I divorced. As a single working mother with a child to provide for, my financial situation had changed drastically. I needed the child support Steve had agreed to pay, but his payments were inconsistent. In fact, he had changed his last name, making it impossible for me to take him to court to offer assistance in enforcing the court-ordered obligation. Although I was frustrated and angry, at the time, I didn't have the emotional fortitude or the financial ability to pursue it. Not only was I experiencing financial hardship, but I also continued my constant battle with drinking.

# Chapter 14

## Staying Stopped

*I* spent the next eight years trying to stop drinking.

My post-divorce life got off to a rocky start. Sean, who was nine years old at the time, and I moved into an apartment in Bayside, Queens. For financial reasons, I had to share the apartment with a roommate with whom I split the rent. I soon realized that she and her boyfriend had a lifestyle that created an unhealthy situation for Sean and me, and I thought it best to find a different place for us to live. We lived there less than a year and then moved to Manhattan. My judgment was so impaired that I couldn't believe I lived there so long.

As a full-time salesperson in a garment center showroom, my job gave us some sense of stability. Even though I was under a great deal of pressure to sell, I was successful, despite my ups and downs. Working full time, I was concerned about Sean's coming home from school to an empty apartment. Fortunately, my dad offered to come to the city to help me out; during the week, he arrived at my apartment in midafternoon when Sean was due home from school and stayed with him until I got home after work. Those times were invaluable and priceless for Sean because his own father wasn't in his life in the way he needed and wanted him to be. In my father he had someone he could confide in, cry to, and express his anger. My gratitude to my parents was strengthened and enhanced.

My career took off, but so did my drinking. I was fortunate that my boss was extremely kind and sympathetic about my efforts to stay stopped. I recall one time when my boss showed me great compassion. He had a liquor cabinet in his office that was filled with bottles of alcohol. One night after work when everyone was gone, I went into his office and drank four bottles of hard liquor. The next morning, he found me sleeping, the empty bottles scattered around me. He confronted me about my drinking, but perhaps because he may have had his own troubles with substances in the past, he offered to pay for me to go to a rehab. Although I didn't take him up on his offer, I have always had a spot in my heart for him.

I was scaring everyone with my drinking. I would embarrass myself and mortify my son and parents. All of my feelings became overwhelming. Under the influence of alcohol, I felt complete and utter hopelessness and despair. I thought my parents and son would be better off without me. I felt that I had only two choices: either kill myself or drink. I thought that the world would be better off because I wasn't a good mother, and I was causing my parents to be unhappy. They had lost a child, and I was drinking myself to death.

In 1979, I tried to take my own life. It was a cry for help. At the time, my son was with my parents at their house. I had reached the point where no matter how much I drank, I could not get drunk anymore. The alcohol was no longer masking anything, not my dread, my despair, or my failure. I took a combination of pills that I obtained from my friends, drank alcohol, and left a note for my son. As I began feeling the effects of the pills and alcohol, I noticed that I was actually free of pain. I called Sean to tell him how much I loved him, and when he heard my voice, he realized something was very wrong, so he called 911. I was rushed to Bellevue Hospital where my stomach was pumped, which was the method used in those days. When I woke up after the procedure, the doctor said, "What are you doing to yourself?" I couldn't admit that I was responsible for the suicide attempt, so I said, "Somebody spiked my drink. I didn't mean to do this." I had to protect my drinking. Believing me, the doctor discharged me. Although I should have, I didn't go to a rehab facility because I thought I could stop drinking on my own.

After I was discharged from the hospital, Steve and my parents conducted an intervention. They begged me to stop destroying myself. They didn't understand why I had attempted suicide. I felt awful hearing how upset my parents were, seeing my parents suffer after having lost a child and then having another child willfully trying to end her life.

Over the years, I went to rehabs, to detox, and to counseling, but I couldn't put ninety days of sobriety together. I would stop for a couple of weeks and then go back to drinking. I even started attending a twelve-step program and had the support of my father, who came to meetings with me and even went to Al-Anon meetings. But for most of eight years I struggled. My objective was always to have just one drink to make my anxiety go away. That's all I wanted. I would tell myself that I would just have one drink, but the drink took me. I struggled, but I couldn't get the message.

I was always looking for that fabulous buzz that alcoholics keep searching for but can no longer get, those early days of blissful happy-go-lucky feelings. But I couldn't sustain it after years of drinking. I have heard fellow recovering alcoholics say that at a certain point, once you have crossed that line, you don't know who is going to show up. That was true of me. When I drank, I took on a different persona. Drinking gave me wings. I was funnier, taller, smarter. On the other hand, I didn't know if I would be the Aviva who was crying, or angry, or flirty, or quiet. I had no way of predicting my behavior. I would tell myself, "When I drink today, I'm not going to make a scene. I'm not going to say my thoughts out loud." But I would have no idea where I would end up and in what condition. My intentions not to drink were always good, but the road to hell is often paved with good intentions.

During these dark times, every emotion I ever had that was suppressed came out when I had too much vodka. My mother was the one who took the brunt of it, causing her to frequently say, "I wish you would have a child like you." When I went into a blackout where I left myself, unaware of my actions or speech, I said some terrible things to her. I expressed my deepest resentments out loud and blamed her for everything that was missing in me. I said,

"Because of you, I'm a worried person." The things I said hurt her badly. Lashing out at her was a huge departure from the behavior of the respectful child that I had been. She would say to my father, "Arnold, there she goes again." She didn't understand that if she had had a different life, I would have had a different life. If someone had shown her that the dance we were doing was so damaging, then she would have done everything to stop it, but neither of us had any awareness of it. Of course, now I forgive her because I realize that she didn't know any better.

During one of the years that I was struggling with my drinking problem, I developed a habit of taking laxatives. I didn't know it then, but I later learned that alcohol addiction and eating disorders frequently occur together in women. To help control my weight and mistakenly thinking that they would help me eliminate the large quantities of alcohol that I was consuming, I took laxatives. I developed a ritual of taking laxatives at a certain time of day, knowing that I couldn't eat anything for a few hours. I also had a ritual for purchasing them. In those days, stores like CVS did not exist, so I had to go to the neighborhood pharmacies. The employees knew me, and I didn't want them to think I had a problem, so I had to plan my trips to many different stores so that I could accumulate enough laxatives to support my excessive use. I even enlisted Sean to buy my ExLax. At one point, I took one hundred laxatives a day. When my program sponsor at the time realized what I had been doing, in fear for my life, she took me to a ward for anorexics in a New York hospital. She said, "I just want you to look around. Some of the girls starved themselves, while others purged." Seeing these emaciated girls hooked up to IVs horrified and frightened me to the point where I immediately tapered off my excessive daily dose of laxatives and eventually stopped taking them altogether.

Although I could not get control of my drinking, I was aware that my behavior was affecting my son, Sean. He witnessed my constant struggle stopping and starting drinking again and my being dishonest about whether I had been drinking or not. When Sean caught me drinking, he would ask,

"What are you doing?" I responded that in my program, I was told that it didn't count if I mixed vodka with seltzer. He knew better. I could see his contempt for me in his face. I saw that look often. In his anger, he retaliated in a big way by getting into trouble. I was constantly worried about him when he wasn't at home, so I hired a limousine service, which I could barely afford, to take him where he wanted to go. This way I knew he would be safe. From the time he was in his early teens, I had an open door policy for his friends. My theory was that I'd rather have him at home than possibly drinking and riding in someone's car.

Even if I wasn't able to help myself, I had enough awareness to realize that I could get help for Sean. I sent him to the Freedom Institute in New York City that offered an Alateen program for children. There he learned how to cope with me, how to hate the disease while not hating me. At a young age, he started getting healthy interpretations and information that kept his heart open rather than shutting it. He was learning to cope with me and not hate me, just hate what I was doing. I am grateful and fortunate that he had all of that outside help. Without it, the ending would have been different.

Throughout the darkest of times, Sean has always been my best friend. He might have been angry, but on some level, he knew that I was not the same person when under the influence of alcohol. He knew that I was a sick person trying to get well, not a bad person.

# Chapter 15

## The Sunlight of the Spirit

*A*fter eight years of numerous attempts at recovery, I was no longer able to tolerate drinking or feel the effects of alcohol. I had had short stretches of sobriety, but I couldn't stay true to my twelve-step program. Even when I attended meetings, I wasn't a truly committed member because I was still drinking. I was in despair.

The trajectory of my life changed significantly in 1988 when Sean, now a teenager in high school, made a bold move that shook me to the core. Because of all of the help that he was getting and from what he had learned from my friends over the years, he knew if I was to have a chance, I needed tough love.

One day, I had been drinking and arguing with Sean. I said, "I'm going to jump off the terrace." I was on the ledge. I had made threats like this every time we had a fight. This time he reacted differently. Rushing onto the terrace, he grabbed me by the lapels of my silk robe and pulled me off the ledge and back onto the terrace. He had never been physical with me before. Pushing me up against the wall, he said, "If you ever do this again in my presence, I will push. I'm done. I cannot do this anymore. I love you, but I will not watch you die." That night, Sean left but said he would stay in touch. For about three weeks, he stayed at his friend's mother's house and slept on the sofa there.

I was devastated. In my inebriated state, I thought that maybe I should go to therapy but continue drinking. Of course, that plan would never solve my problem. Then, something shifted in me. I needed to talk to Sean eye to eye, face to face, and do it without a drink and with a therapist present. In order to impress Sean with my new resolution, I made an appointment with a family therapist, thinking that I could convince Sean that I was ready to get well. I didn't have the courage to meet with him without a drink, so I drank in the cab on my way to see them but was not drunk when I arrived. After therapy that same night, he agreed to come home with me where we had a heart-to-heart talk. In despair, I said, "You are the only thing that matters to me, and now I've lost you. I've lost everything." Once again, Sean said, "I cannot stand by and watch you die."

Sean's words catapulted me into action. My fear of losing him caused me to check into a rehab facility. The women I saw there looked like me, quite normal on the outside, but all of us had eyes that had no light. I knew my family loved me. Why couldn't I stop drinking? I came to realize that love is not enough. Willpower is not enough. No human power will ever be enough to keep someone sober.

During my twenty-eight days in rehab, I heard powerful words from three speakers who had come to the rehab center as a form of service. I was struck by their generosity and so moved by their message that I was inspired that night to fervently pray to God to help me recover and clear whatever was blocking me. For the first time, I said, "I can't do this anymore." I got down on my knees, crying for help. In that one moment, I felt an unbelievable sense of peace and hope. My desire to drink was lifted in that instant. I was a woman who drank in the morning, who had liquor in her purse and hidden in her boots, who had numerous ways to conceal her liquor bottles. And in one instant, as I prayed, the thought of drinking vanished. Nothing before that moment had worked: no threats of losing my marriage or having my son leave, hurting my parents, or losing my job. Nothing was in the way. I felt complete surrender, truly knowing that I was not in charge. It was up to me to accept the outcome. I prayed for strength, acceptance, and guidance. I believed that God was in charge, and all I could ask for was the strength to carry out His wishes. When I realized that it wasn't up to me, I felt freedom. I was committed to my higher power.

January 16, 1988, marked my first day of sobriety. My spiritual experience catapulted me into a new reality. I completed treatment, and when I came out, I began a new life and a new journey without alcohol or any mind-altering chemicals for the next nineteen years. My recovery took more than love. For me it had to be something profound that shook me to my core. Some people have a gradual recovery by going through the steps of a program or having a spiritual experience. I had to do both. The spiritual awakening was just enough to be the catalyst. The first moment it happened, I still had the same problems: work, financial, single motherhood. Still, I didn't drink. Everything was the same in my life. The only thing that changed was that I wasn't drinking. I genuinely thought God chose me.

Looking back, I recalled with a new awareness all the chances I had taken when I had been drinking, not only with my life, but with my loved ones' lives and possibly those of people I didn't know. I thought about all the money I wasted, all the harm I caused to myself and others.

I had had so many experiences when I was under the influence where I could have died. More than once I almost fell off the train platform onto the tracks. I was involved in car accidents, in particular, one in which I went through the windshield. I always drove drunk with my son or parents in the car. Somehow, I was saved numerous times from falling asleep with a lit cigarette, or from erratically crossing the street without paying attention and yet not getting hit by a car. I felt that I was being looked after, that I had God's angels around me.

Doctors, friends, and family had told me many times that I was going to die, have a heart attack, or have my kidneys shut down if I didn't stop drinking. I drank such massive quantities of liquor, a quart or two of vodka every day, that it was remarkable that I didn't need to have a liver transplant, that my organs still worked, that I didn't have a wet brain. I was alive and sober only because of the prayers of others.

From the moment I had my awakening, I stayed sober for a long time. I was faithful to my recovery program. I enjoyed every aspect of my new life:

traveling, attending seminars, and participating in presentations with a group from my recovery program. My new friends were committed to being sober, and we developed long-lasting relationships; we socialized together, attended the opera, the ballet, and parties. I also met someone special who had a strong influence over my recovery, and we had great respect for one another.

Around my ninth year of sobriety, Sean met Tammi, who was to become my daughter-in-law. I was thrilled that Sean had found someone with strong family values and maintained a close relationship with her parents. Although some single mothers might have been unhappy about losing a son to marriage, I knew that Sean would be in good hands, and I was glad to share him. Tammi knew that Sean and I had a close relationship, so out of respect and with a kind heart, she invited me on many of their outings. Sean brought Tammi to our Sunday brunches at my parents' house, where my parents got to know her, embracing her as part of the family. I could see that Sean and Tammi were a perfect fit. With great joy, I started to imagine how different my life would now be with Tammi in the picture. As a result, I threw myself into recovery even more.

For me, the only power that will ever keep me sober and come between me and a drink is a power greater than myself. That's what I found at the rehab center. I call that power God. I had to have complete reliance on that power. I had to ask that power for help. And I still ask that power for help even today. I doubt that my recovery would have been possible, though, without Sean, who I believe God sent as a messenger. He has and always will be my angel.

# Chapter 16

## Lucky

$\mathcal{A}$fter so many years of struggle and then recovery, I had hoped that one day I would find love. My wish came true when I met Kenny on May 5, 1999, and began a new chapter in my life. I had been invited to a party where one of our fellowship members, Perry, was celebrating his recovery birthday on his real birthday. Of course, none of us were drinking alcohol. In fact, I had been sober for ten years and was extremely proud of my accomplishment. The only "outsider" at the party was Kenny, Perry's friend with whom he had grown up. During this event, I was told that Kenny was smitten with me, that he couldn't stop looking at me. Little did I know at the time how much my life was going to change.

My relationship with Kenny began gradually in May with phone calls. Not long after, we had our first date, which took place at a little jewel of a chef-owned and operated restaurant called Firenze. The twinkling lights, unique flowers, and a single lit candle on our table set the stage for a memorable, romantic evening. Although neither of us had planned to, we found the setting conducive to sharing our deepest, darkest secrets. I felt that it was important to tell Kenny about my past and that my family and my sobriety would always come first. I advised, "If you ever see me acting strangely or just not behaving like myself, call my sponsor because I may be approaching trouble." I was concerned that learning about my past would deter Kenny from moving forward with our relationship, but fortunately, it didn't seem to matter to him.

Our second date took place on Kenny's birthday. I was hesitant about accepting the invitation because I wasn't sure if he was right for me, but my sponsor Peggy encouraged me to go. She also suggested that I buy him a whimsical, lighthearted gift because that was the right thing to do even if I didn't know Kenny well yet. I was not sure what kind of gift would be appropriate, so I browsed at a store that was a block from my apartment. While there, a tan baseball cap with the word *lucky* embroidered across the front struck me as the perfect present. The color was neutral and wearable, but most importantly, I thought the message on the hat was fun. As it turned out, he loved it. This cap soon became a symbol of how lucky we were to have found each other. In fact, I still have the cap after all these years.

When I arrived at the restaurant for Kenny's birthday dinner, I was pleasantly surprised to find out that Kenny's family had been invited. For so long I had what I would call a hunger for family because my immediate family was so small, my parents having lost most of their relatives during the Holocaust. I met Kenny's son Taylor, his sister, niece, and cousins. What a lovely family, I thought. I was in family heaven.

As I got to know Kenny better, I became aware of his many admirable qualities. He loved to have fun, to entertain, and to share with others. When someone he cared about needed financial help, he unselfishly gave it, even though he didn't have unlimited funds. Kenny was the one who generously picked up the check when we went out to dinner with friends, and he never expected them to reciprocate. Not only did he love to shop for food, cook, and eat, but he was comfortable in the kitchen. In fact, on his boat that had a tiny galley, he could cook up a six-course dinner for twelve people, including pasta and lobster.

Kenny's effect on me was life changing. By October, Kenny asked me to move in with him. He had a beautiful apartment overlooking the New York City skyline with extended views to the south, east, and west to Fifth Avenue. As tempting as his offer was, I wasn't completely convinced that I was ready to take such a big step. I had all kinds of excuses. For instance, I said, "How can I move in? I have a cat. You have two dogs." Kenny replied, "Don't worry. They'll like each other." He took that problem off my list. In his effort to further persuade me, one day he invited me to his apartment so that we could continue our discussion about my moving in. When I arrived, Kenny was beaming with pride as he ushered me to the bathroom to show me that he had purchased the same brands of creams, perfumes, soaps, and bathrobe that he observed at my apartment. This gesture showed me how thoughtful he was and how much he wanted me to feel at home with him. Soon thereafter, I moved in. Every day, I would pinch myself and say, "Oh, God, please let me keep what I have." I began to believe that Kenny was "the one."

Not long after I moved in with Kenny, he asked me to go on a sailing trip with him on a chartered boat. He loved to sail, but I was reluctant because I hadn't been on a boat since I came to the United States so many years ago and had vivid memories of being seasick for weeks. Although I didn't want to experience seasickness again, I knew how much he loved sailing and wanted me to enjoy it with him. Because Kenny was a solution-oriented person, he came up with an idea to find out whether or not I would still get seasick. He took me to some floating docks on Long Island where I could experience the movement of the water without stepping onto a boat. Discovering that I didn't get seasick put wind in our sails.

We set sail in a beautiful boat with a galley and staterooms. At each port, Kenny arranged for relatives or friends to meet us. We would sail together for two days, drop one group off at another port, and pick up others to join us at different ports, each with its own charm. My love for him was increasing every day.

Our relationship moved forward, and we grew closer. When Kenny met my family, he embraced them as if they were his own blood. My parents adored him too and were so happy that I was in a relationship with someone who loved and cared about me, but they had a strong desire to see me married so that they wouldn't have to worry about my being alone. Actually, while I enjoyed living with Kenny, I wanted to get married because for me, marriage symbolized a deeper commitment to our relationship. I started to hint to Kenny that even though I was happy with our current arrangement, living together indefinitely was not an option. On the other hand, Kenny felt that the commitment had already been made when he asked me to move in. In his mind, we were married; we already had grown children, so there was no point to it. I think he would rather have chewed on broken glass than get married again. But I continued to ask, and he would say, "When the time is right." I kept waiting for the right time to come.

One day, Kenny and I were having dinner at one of our favorite restaurants, Scales, in Newport, Rhode Island. After dinner, we took a stroll in the shopping district and came across a jewelry store. Knowing how much I loved jewelry, we went in to admire the unique items. There I saw a beautiful, modern style ring with an aquamarine stone set on a gold band. I whispered to Kenny, "You know, I don't need a diamond to get engaged. Hint. Hint." My comment having no apparent effect, we left the store without the ring. Without my knowing, Kenny secretly managed to go back to the store without me and bought the ring. The days went by, and I had forgotten about the ring.

Not long after that, Kenny and I went on another one of our sailing trips, this time to Nantucket. My boss and his wife had joined us for that part of the trip, and they knew that Kenny had planned something special for me. One morning at sunrise, Kenny woke me up and asked me to come on deck. With the sun beginning to light the sky, Kenny got down on one knee and proposed, placing the ring, the one I had admired in Nantucket, on my finger. Kenny's flair for romance and surprise continued not long after. A few weeks after our trip, I walked into the large lobby of our apartment building where I saw dozens of white roses on a table. I asked Jack, the doorman, who the roses were for, and he told me they were for someone new in the building. I went up to our twenty-eighth floor apartment where Kenny was waiting. A few minutes later, the doorbell rang, and porters carried all those roses I had seen in the lobby into our apartment. They had been for me! Kenny always found unique ways to surprise me.

Kenny and I got married on May 20, 2000. The ceremony was conducted in Temple Sharay Tefila where we had attended some sabbath services and had become friendly with the rabbi. After the ceremony, we held a luncheon at Firenze, the intimate restaurant where we had our first date. We reserved the entire restaurant and invited our closest family members and friends, an intimate crowd which made it easy to socialize. A guitarist and violinist provided background music, which created a calming effect in contrast with the jovial, celebratory mood of the participants. Of all the toasts and congratulations, Sean's tribute was especially meaningful and memorable. He read a letter that he had written for the occasion, which traced my journey over the years from his perspective, spanning his childhood to my recovery and to the person I had become. So touching was his letter that all of the guests were moved, some wiping tears from their eyes. On that special day, with all the love and support we were blessed with, I believed I finally had everything I had ever wanted.

# Chapter 17

## Death Grip

$\mathcal{B}$eing married to Kenny provided financial security, safety, and fun, but more importantly, it provided love. While he worked during the day, I went to daytime recovery program meetings. He didn't mind when I went to an hour meeting several blocks from our apartment, but I began to think that I needed to be available for Kenny. He was taking care of me, making my life better. I needed to repay him with all my free time.

Gradually, over a period of four years of my marriage to Kenny, I stopped dedicating my life to recovery. I cut back on the number of meetings I attended even though I knew from experience that meetings were instrumental in keeping a person sober. I started to make excuses to myself: "Of course I can go on a boat trip for four weeks," or "It's raining. I'll just call somebody instead of going to a meeting." At first, I would take one day off a week. Then, I would miss two meetings a week. After a few months passed, I started to miss three meetings and arrived late to the ones I did attend. Not only did I attend fewer meetings, but also I stopped taking phone calls from or making calls to others in the program. Calling people is one of the responsibilities to connect to others and to be available when others connect with us. When people start to cut back or stop doing those things, they are getting closer to drinking again.

I started to think that I was in charge. After all my years in my program, I thought, I've got this. I know the tools. I know I'm not going to drink. I don't need to waste my time going to those "stupid" meetings. I can recite all the principles and steps. I was beginning to think that my higher power was no longer God; it was Kenny.

Without the support of meetings, a sponsor, or fellowship, I wasn't living the recovery lifestyle. I wasn't connected to other people who understood the disease of alcoholism; I didn't stay in the middle of the herd. I knew that when an alcoholic was isolated from the group, she would have a greater chance of relapse, but I ignored this warning that was desperately trying to get my attention. People say when you stop going to meetings, eventually, you will pick up a drink. I couldn't live on yesterday's recovery.

My strength and confidence started to diminish, and I reverted to being broken but without alcohol. I started to lose myself, to slowly recede from the person I had become. I began to tolerate things that I would not have considered acceptable before. I gave Kenny the power to influence how I felt; I relied on his mood. If he was happy, I was happy. If he was unhappy, I was unhappy. His stress became my stress. Despite all of Kenny's wonderful qualities, on occasion, Kenny would lose his temper. He was able recover in ten minutes, but in my fragile emotional state, I couldn't express myself and kept my feelings inside.

Without the protection of all the meetings, all of the support network, and my belief in a higher power, I experienced a "feeling." Having feelings that were too much for me was the reason I drank to begin with. So much was out of place with me. My feelings were unmanageable. If I had been attending meetings, I could have worked through them; I would have been sharing them. I had been keeping my feelings to myself, and I was susceptible to "going out," and that's exactly what happened.

After all those years of sobriety, it didn't matter what I had learned. I had left my God. I could say that it was because my mother was ill, which brought up all of those old feelings, but that was not true. I drank because I was no longer a member in good standing, and I no longer was praying in the same way that I had prayed before for help. Instead, I thanked God for the things that being with Kenny had brought me: Thank you God for this beautiful panoramic view of the city. Please don't ever take it away from me. Thank you for this beautiful furniture. I put things first. So I had to learn the hard way. I left the protection of my higher power and became susceptible to harming myself in some way permanently. I didn't have my higher power to help me from making bad decisions.

The disease of alcoholism is always talking. It had me in its grip once again. I chose to drink rather than call a recovery friend to talk me off the ledge. At that moment, I wanted to drink more than I wanted to be sober. I was no longer able to resist, so I went to a liquor store and bought a bottle of vodka, came home, and drank. Initially, the vodka assuaged my anxiety, but I couldn't enjoy the buzz because guilt took over. I was shocked at my behavior because I knew better.

At first, I had no intention of telling Kenny, but when he came home from work that day, I blurted out, "I drank." He wasn't upset with me, but he was as shocked as I was. He said, "What? Are you kidding?" Then he remembered that I had told him on our first date that if he saw me acting strangely, he should call my sponsor. With me present, Kenny called her. We knew that I needed to go back to rehab, and we searched for a rehab that would be right for me.

In the beginning of my return to drinking, Kenny felt so bad. He would ask what he could do to help. I tried to convince him that I was drinking because my hair was falling out to the point where I was going to be bald or because my mother wasn't well. I even agreed to go to rehab to keep my son and my parents off my back, but my mother got very sick and was hospitalized, so I was allowed to leave the facility. I wasn't devoted to recovery.

From then on, I went in and out of treatment centers. I started doing some of the things I had learned in my program: counting the days that I didn't drink, calling my sponsor, and going to meetings. The meetings didn't help because I just wasn't fully present; I was just attending. Clearly, I wasn't committed. I hadn't changed sufficiently and was still thinking that I was managing my drinking. This slip began a series of years going in and out. I had gone through two detoxes and three rehabs, but at all of those rehabs, I didn't connect with my higher power. I would go and feel some encouragement that I was going to achieve recovery. I had all the right intentions, but I wasn't willing to take the first step, which is to admit defeat.

The disease had me in its grip, literally and figuratively. One specific humiliating incident shows just how out of control I had become. Kenny found me drunk one day and called my friend, who then called my support network. When they arrived at our house, they witnessed a desperate scene. I was on my knees, licking the floor, which was scattered with shattered glass from the bottle of vodka I had dropped. I was attempting to lap up every last drop of vodka that had spilled. Then I grabbed another bottle, and knowing my friends would try to take it from me, I held onto it in what my friend called a death grip because I refused to release it. In my desperation, I tried to bite her because she was trying to stop me from taking my next gulp of alcohol. I would have done anything to get it.

After my mother died, I became a fall down drunk. I never asked for help and rarely went to meetings. I was walking into a landmine. I had started to drink and go into blackouts. My husband had married a sober woman, but when I started drinking again, he didn't know who I was. I couldn't get back to sobriety. Echoes of the statements Steve, my first husband, had made resonated when Kenny said, "I didn't sign up for this." His opinion of me had changed, and he was angry. He didn't understand the disease, that I didn't want to be drinking, that I had lost my way, and his behavior wasn't helping.

I had become a danger to myself and others. One day, while driving, I went into a blackout and found myself on someone's lawn. I got out of the car and fell, with part of my body landing under the car. I was very drunk, but God was with me again. The police were called, and fortunately, when they arrived at the scene, I didn't get a DWI because the car keys weren't in my hand. I was taken to the hospital by ambulance where Kenny was waiting for me, having been alerted by the police that I would be brought there. Of course, he was upset and worried, even more so when I kept repeating that I wanted to die, so I was assigned a female nurse to stand guard in my room. I didn't want to be there; I wanted a drink. So I waited for her to fall asleep, snuck out of the hospital, and immediately hailed a cab. I asked the driver to stop at a liquor store, but to my consternation, it was closed. I desperately needed alcohol, so I bought two bottles of vanilla because they contained alcohol and drank the contents. In my disheveled state, wearing dirty clothes and feeling emotionally fragile, I went to my father's house. Understandably, he was quite upset to see me in this condition, so reminiscent of my behavior and struggles in the past.

A few months later, my drinking while driving caused another incident that landed me in the hospital. I had borrowed a friend's car and went into a blackout, side swiping a few cars. I came out of the blackout after I had hit the last car and pulled into my friend's garage. I clearly remember the garage attendant's reaction, looking at me and at then at the car and shaking his head. I felt pathetic and embarrassed. When I arrived at my apartment building, the doorman regarded me with concern as I walked by because he had never seen me in that state before. As I rode up on the elevator to my apartment, I fell flat on my face, breaking my nose and knocking out several teeth, causing two black eyes. Once again, I found myself in an ambulance being taken to an emergency room, then a hospital room with a nurse assigned to guard me. I was humiliated. As soon as I was discharged, I immediately went to a bar; it was 11 a.m. I had never gone to bars, was never a bar drinker, but lacking enough money to buy a bottle of vodka, I was able to buy that much needed drink. My moment of reckoning was soon to come.

When Kenny and I were visiting Sean and Tammi to celebrate my granddaughter's fifth birthday, Sean took one look at me and knew I had been drinking. He said, "Ma, you're drunk, and it's Sarah's birthday. How could you do this?" He didn't turn me away, but warned, "You had better not do anything to ruin it. I will send you home if you do something embarrassing." I was nervous when I entered their home because I did not want to spoil her party. Sarah took one look at me and said, "Grandma Vivi, how come you're only smiling with your mouth and not with your eyes?" My smile didn't seem sincere to her because she had seen me in the past when I was sober and knew what I looked like when I was smiling and happy. Her statement was devastating for me to hear. It broke my heart that my granddaughter was able to look into my soul and see the darkness there, my eyes devoid of any joy. I didn't stay very long because I was nervous; I couldn't rely on my thinking process.

Shortly thereafter, on a Sunday night, Kenny found me drinking beer in the garage of our second home in Florida. I never drank beer, but Kenny had given all the alcohol in the house away to the neighbors to make it difficult for me to drink, so there wasn't anything else alcoholic except beer. I was humiliated because I felt that he was disclosing to the neighbors that his wife couldn't be around liquor. He agreed that he wouldn't tell Sean that I had been drinking, but he insisted that the incident be a one-time thing. But I didn't—couldn't stop. The next day, I was still drinking. At around 12 p.m., Kenny said, "I'm leaving on a 6 o'clock flight to go back to New York. I can't be around you."

Just like on the television show *Intervention*, Kenny, Sean, and Tammi conducted their own intervention with me. They said, "If you can't help yourself, then you can stay the way you are." Tammi said she would Baker Act me because I was a harm to myself and others. They took my car keys so that I couldn't drive because I had been driving under the influence.

The next day somebody called my sponsor, who put us in touch with a liaison between patients and rehabs. She suggested Challenges in Ft. Lauderdale because it wasn't too far from our home in Wellington, about forty-five minutes away. I could have visitors on the weekends. Once again, I agreed to go because of my desire to please and get my family off my back.

# Chapter 18

## The Light at the End of the Tunnel

When I sobered up after my family's intervention and realized that I had agreed to go to rehab, I was freaked out. I had told Kenny and Sean that I would go, so backing out was too much for me to bear. I knew that if I didn't go and get sober again, they would all temporarily abandon me, which would be devastating.

Sean drove me to Challenges, the treatment center in Ft. Lauderdale that had been recommended. When he dropped me off, he looked directly at me and said, "Mom, tell them everything." Somehow, he knew that I had many secrets and was guarding them too much. His statement was powerful, the key to open the door. I always had secrets and compartments that I had never dealt with because of my shame, guilt, and fear of being found out, judged, and then abandoned.

As was my frame of mind so many times before, I wasn't serious about recovery. In my alcoholic conniving mind, I had a plan to allow me to continue to drink and take pills while I was there. My intention was to bring airplane-size bottles of vodka hidden in the stuffing of a decorative pillow. I would also bring a small number of pills, Xanax and Klonopin, which I had accumulated from friends over time, tucked into one of my socks. No one at rehab would check any of these items, so I would be able to fortify myself if needed. To execute this plan, I recruited a friend to buy the mini bottles of alcohol. Then, I opened up the seam of the decorative pillow and positioned the bottles deep inside the stuffing. I didn't know how to sew the seam closed, so I brought the pillow to the tailor to sew it. To my disappointment, I learned that the pillow wasn't ready in time, so I couldn't take it with me to rehab. My plan had been ruined, but not being able to drink while there turned out to be a blessing, another God miracle.

I showed up at Challenges with a wardrobe that I immediately learned was out of place. I didn't know that this particular rehab was not like some of upscale centers where I had received treatment in the past. With my long, flowing dresses and skirts hanging out of the bottom of my garment bag that was made for men's suits, too short for my clothes, I looked ridiculous. When a few of the residents of the rehab who were sitting in chairs on the lawn saw me, they looked at each other and joked, "We've got a live one." I soon realized no one dressed up there. I thought if I looked good on the outside, maybe I could fool people into believing that I was good on the inside. However, in the end, the way I or anyone else dressed was irrelevant.

During the first few days in rehab, I was just marking time. As residents, we attended meetings every day either on or off the premises to listen to speakers who offered support and inspiration. After the speaker was finished, we were encouraged to thank him or her. Sometimes, too many people were waiting to chat with the speaker, so saying more than thank you wasn't possible. On this particular day, however, I had an opportunity. I explained to the speaker, "I don't know why I can't stop drinking. I really don't want to drink. I don't understand why I can't stop. I've tried so many things." Then he asked me one question: "Are you giving it away? Are you passing it on?" I told him that I wasn't. He replied, "Well, you have to. You can't keep it unless you give it away. It's that paradox." When I heard this gentleman asking if I had worked with others, I realized that I hadn't, and I made a commitment that if I ever got sober, I was going to dedicate myself to work with others, "to pass it on."

That brief conversation was life-altering. I realized that I couldn't do just one thing, whether it was just going to meetings, or working with others, or fellowship. I had to do all of it. I wanted to feel joy, to have self-esteem, to feel worthy, but especially, I wanted to feel that I was giving back because of what was so freely given to me by strangers who went out of their way to help me. I realized that while I had dedicated myself to parts of the program, I had my own version, my recipe, the way I chose to apply the program. I used to tell my sponsor, "My program isn't working," and she would say, "Try ours." I became aware that if you want to use someone else's recipe, but you change it, and you can't figure out why it doesn't taste the same, it's because you didn't follow the recipe.

Finally, in this place, at that moment in time, I truly felt that I was chosen to have another chance. I knew it, felt it, and I became totally dedicated. I was meticulous about journaling, and it was then that I started to write this autobiography.

Among the many breakthroughs I had during my stay in rehab, my choice to remove my hair extensions was monumental. Over the years, I had lost a lot of hair from those early days of not eating, so from the age of thirty, I have always worn hair extensions in public. As I progressed through my program, I had reached the fifth step, which involves talking to another person and sharing your deepest, darkest secrets. I shared everything with all the women in the group emotionally and spiritually. Suddenly, I was motivated to take an action that I would never have done in the past; I removed my extensions. The next day, I realized that by taking my extensions off, I had revealed myself physically, laid bare all my secrets.

The most magical thing for me was that Kenny flew down to Florida from New York on visiting day. I was thrilled to see him and overjoyed when he decided to stay in Florida for the duration of the time I had left in rehab. Every weekend, Kenny came to visit me, surprising me with flowers. When I was discharged from rehab and got my phone back, which had been confiscated, I found messages that Kenny had left specifically for the time when I could listen to them.

When I came out of rehab, for the first time in my life, I felt that there was a solution, and it was available to me if I was willing to do the work. I had hope that I could truly do this. I gained more confidence in myself and had a better view of reality, a better view of who I was, and I was no longer giving other people the power to determine my happiness. I thank God every single day that Challenges was in existence. The people gathered in that place at that moment in time reached me in a way that I had never experienced.

I've heard it said before, but I heard it more loudly this time that when you are in a treatment center, if you look to the person on your right and on your left, they might not be there tomorrow. You have to really want to succeed because there are so many obstacles to overcome to stay stopped. In fact, now, of all the women who were in our group at rehab, only one other person and I have stayed sober.

I had nineteen years of sobriety, and I've had hell years in between. I've been sober since I left Challenges in 2009. I am an alcoholic in recovery with no shame. I believe that the people who get sober in spite of their demons can help other people understand that they can survive an emotion without a pill or a drink or a drug. I have known the joy of giving back by helping a person make the connection, by seeing the lights come on in someone else's discovery. By giving, I get more.

I know now, and I've known for a long time, that I can have feelings, and they won't kill me.

# Chapter 19

## Resilience

*I*n 2009, I had completed the program at Challenges and was newly sober. I knew that my experience there was life altering; I had breakthroughs that I had never achieved in any other treatment program. I had become a stronger, more confident person. I knew that I was in recovery, but my sobriety was to be tested by so many unexpected circumstances and obstacles.

When I first came home after rehab, Kenny and I had a difficult time rebuilding trust. I had put Kenny through so much that at first, he had a hard time accepting that I was really sober and committed to recovery. For my part, I was filled with remorse over the disruption I had caused in our lives. Eventually, over time, we both came to terms with all that had happened.

A few years later, our lives came crashing down on us. The trouble started in 2012. Kenny's industry had started to decline due to product saturation. With increased competition and price wars, some companies were using illegal business practices. Complaints were filed, leading to the government's investigation of the industry across the country. Businesses were accused and convicted of *enticement*, a legal term meaning "to wrongfully solicit, persuade, procure, allure, attract, coax, or seduce, or to lure, induce, attempt, incite, or persuade a person to do a thing." As a result, many businesses were closed down.

To our surprise and apprehension, we learned that Kenny was being investigated, followed by an indictment not long after. Kenny's son Taylor, who had recently come on board as a manager in Kenny's business, had been running the company because Kenny had been recovering from back surgery and was working from our Florida home. In Kenny's absence, a recently hired salesman, who was actually an informant, secretly recorded Kenny's employees. Apparently, Taylor had said something that was sufficient to incriminate him, which led to his indictment. In addition, all of the salesmen were indicted.

Our money and our lives were on a downward spiral. We immediately hired criminal attorneys who assured us that Kenny's company's contracts contained the appropriate disclaimers. Although Kenny was still permitted to operate his company, business was bad, so our income decreased. The decline in Kenny's business and the five hundred dollar an hour lawyers' fees were a huge drain on our finances. Kenny and I did our best to support each other and give each other strength during this disturbing time in our lives. Kenny was afraid I would drink, and I was afraid that he would have a heart attack. Despite our troubles, I was hopeful, refusing to believe that God would take Kenny from me.

Kenny had made an arrangement with his lawyer to turn himself in voluntarily if an arrest was imminent, and that is what he did. However, Taylor was taken by surprise when he was arrested at 5:30 in the morning. We then learned and that both Kenny and Taylor were to go on trial together. They sat side by side in the courtroom and had the same judge and jury.

From the beginning of the trial to the final verdict, I accompanied Kenny, hoping that my presence in the courtroom would provide much needed emotional support. Every morning, at around 7:15 a.m., Kenny and I would leave our apartment and ride down in the elevator to the garage in our building. Actually, I used to go down a short time before Kenny and ask for the car to be pulled up. Then, Kenny would come down a minute or two later. Courtney, the attendant, noticed how grim, intense, and sad we looked every morning when we left. He never knew what we were going through, but he knew something terrible was happening. In the moments I waited for Kenny to join me in the garage, Courtney took me aside, and holding both of my hands in his, he said a prayer for me, and then we prayed together. I knew that God had put an angel in my life in the form of Courtney. I took that prayer moment with me all day while I sat in court. The power of these prayers helped give me strength through the trial and with my anxiety about the outcome.

I also derived some degree of solace during the trial by focusing on the words "In God We Trust," prominently emblazoned on the wall behind the judge. My faith that we would be taken care of was strong. I always believed that Kenny and Taylor would be found innocent, but as the trial progressed, my confidence began to waver. I was sick to my stomach every day and chain smoked even though I was not a smoker. Not being able to hide my emotions very well, I received constant warnings from Kenny's attorneys to stop glowering at the judge and prosecutor. My anger was ignited when I heard all the ugly, untrue, highly exaggerated misinformation about Kenny and his business. To my horror, I began to see that the U.S. Department of Justice could make the truth seem like a lie. Kenny's salesmen, who had also been indicted, had banded together and made similar statements, accusing Kenny of wrong-doing and lying about his involvement.

Seeing people in attendance looking at me and judging me, thinking I was a part of it too, was unpleasant and demoralizing. I had to listen to the judge damage Kenny by implication, guide the jury to ignore certain information, and deny our attorneys' objections. Every day I sat in the courtroom behind Kenny and Taylor, their backs hunched over. I sensed their tension and fears, saw their bodies physically react to the words that were untrue, their shoulders drooping, heads falling forward as their characters were slaughtered.

We observed that the judge seemed to seek the jury's favor. For instance, on a rainy day, she would say, "You know, it's raining. Why don't we end early?" She even ordered Chinese food for them. Whatever she said or did made her a hero to the jury. She was successful at swaying the jury by her objections and the way she led the prosecutor. For example, she suggested to the prosecutor, "I don't think you want to ask that question." Often gasps were engendered from the people in the courtroom who had come to support us when they heard the judge's egregious directions and comments. We began to think that the prosecutor and the judge were in an alliance, though we could never prove it. We learned that the prosecutor and judge assigned to our case had agendas unrelated to the case, that the prosecutor was going to lose her job and that the judge was hoping to get a Supreme Court position, so she needed a large number of convictions. In addition, the justice department and the district attorney's offices were instructed to convict Kenny.

I didn't believe that Kenny would be convicted because we had so much evidence in his favor. We were shocked when the jury handed down a guilty verdict. With my heart pounding, barely breathing, feeling completely numb, I heard the word *guilty*. Taylor was sentenced first, then Kenny. Words cannot describe all of the emotions I felt for Kenny, Taylor, and me at that moment. I was terrified. Our lives were completely shattered. At the end of the trial, Taylor was sentenced to seven years for a crime he had not committed. Adding to our horror at his sentence was the court's instruction that Taylor remove his belt, tie, and shoes in front of everyone in the courtroom, an action that is usually done privately. Kenny was devastated, not only with Taylor's sentence, but also with his own sentence of fourteen years.

Lies and unsubstantiated accusations led to what we felt was an unfair trial. Our attorneys believed Kenny to be innocent and found numerous grounds for appeal, but it was not to happen. He had told me before the trial that if he was convicted, he would never go to jail. "I will never go to jail. In my seventies with my kidney, neck, and back problems, I will not sleep on a cot and have to eat terrible food. You have to be prepared that if I am convicted, I'm not going," he insisted. He would have been in his late eighties at the completion of a fourteen-year sentence. After his sentencing, he reaffirmed that he would not go to jail. I couldn't imagine how this was possible. I insisted, "We'll get through this. We'll get an appeal. God would never take you from me." As the days went on until sentencing, Kenny's eyes looked different; they looked dead, like he wasn't there. His skin took on a gray pallor. His deterioration was unbearable for me to watch.

Kenny had agreed to turn himself in, in two weeks, but once again, we were in for another shock. The judge decided to issue a bench warrant, which meant that Kenny could be picked up at any time. In the two weeks we thought we had been given, we had planned to help Taylor get his affairs in order since he had been taken directly to jail from the courtroom. Despite the bench warrant looming over us, we decided to move forward. We knew it was risky to leave our apartment, wondering if the FBI or U.S. Marshalls were waiting for us in the lobby, but we didn't feel that we had a choice. In order to avoid being seen on an elevator in our building with Kenny's medications and our luggage, we quietly descended twenty-eight flights of stairs. Our first destination was Taylor's condo, where we would take his two dogs and move his car out of his condo's garage so that he wouldn't have to pay for parking while he was in jail. After that, I would drive Taylor's car to Kenny's niece's house in Rockland County, a suburb of New York, and Kenny would drive his own car and meet me there. The drive to Taylor's was nerve-wracking; we had to remove our E-ZPass, an automated toll collection system, and turn off our phones so we couldn't be tracked.

After successfully accomplishing those tasks, we arrived at his niece's house, where we planned to stay for a couple of weeks until Kenny was to be picked up. What happened next was so unexpected that even to this day, I find it difficult to talk about. After the trial ended, Kenny's heart was broken. His knew his beloved son Taylor was going to jail for something he did not do. The stress of the trial, the loss of his business, the publicity, Taylor's imprisonment, and the injustice of it all had been weighing on his heart. But I never expected to wake up in the morning and find my beloved husband lying dead next to me. I was in shock, disbelief. I couldn't process it. My eyes were drawn to the night table next to his side of the bed where Kenny always kept his medications. I noticed that one of the bottles was completely empty, which was unusual because he always kept his prescriptions up-to-date. I didn't know what to think. His niece and I called the coroner, who confirmed that Kenny had died from a heart attack.

All of a sudden, I was alone, no longer a part of a couple. Kenny had been in charge of our finances, so I didn't know much about them. I was aware that we had depleted our resources by paying lawyers' fees, so in order to pay for Kenny's funeral, I had to borrow money from Sean. Sean and Tammi flew to New York to help me sort through all of Kenny's paperwork. At first, we thought that Kenny had not made sufficient provisions for me, but after reading the trust, Sean figured out that he had. I was told that I couldn't remain in our apartment because I would use up all of the money Kenny had left me, but I knew I couldn't leave New York right away because I had so many responsibilities. I had Kenny's legal fees to pay and Taylor's attorney to deal with. I didn't have time to mourn.

Taylor was released on bail a few months later, and, eventually, his conviction was overturned. He used his inheritance from his father to buy a business, which was well-suited to his talents. He seemed to be on a trajectory to a better life. Knowing that I planned to relocate to Florida where my son and his family lived, Taylor asked if he could live in our apartment; he wanted to reside where he was raised and someday raise a family. I was concerned about overseeing the apartment from out of town, so we drew up an agreement, requiring him to pay me a year's rent up front. Taylor had been living in that apartment for only a few months when another tragedy occurred. One day, out of the blue, Taylor's girlfriend called me crying, "I can't wake him up. I can't wake him up." Taylor had died from an accidental drug overdose at the age of thirty-six. I knew he was troubled, always looking to find inner peace and happiness, and unfortunately, he used substances to reach for that. He had been a tortured soul, and even with all the material things he had, he was still empty inside so that nothing could bring him happiness. I had always wondered if that apartment was bad luck because Kenny's first wife died there, Taylor died there, my cat fell off the 28th floor terrace, and two dogs died, one of them tragically.

In just a few months, Kenny and Taylor had been convicted and sentenced, Kenny died, Taylor died, and I moved to Florida. I had hoped to continue my relationship with Kenny's relatives. Over the years of my marriage to Kenny, I was thrilled to be part of an extended family. However, when Kenny's sister learned that Kenny had not left her any inheritance, which she had expected, she turned some of the family members against me, and all contact was severed. In just a few months, my entire family through marriage was lost.

So much had happened to change my life in such a short period of time. If anyone had told me that I would have to undergo all of this while sober, I would not have believed it. Yet through it all, I did not drink. I had promised my son and daughter-in-law that I would do everything I could to avoid falling back. There were times when I could have weakened, but my resolve and my commitment to my higher power, that promise I had made, was so important to me that I was sustained by it. Drinking wouldn't have undone anything that I had lost and would have actually caused greater losses. No event can make you drink. You can get through anything, and no matter what, you don't drink. Over the years, I have said that if my parents could survive the Holocaust, then I can survive whatever comes my way in my journey through life.

# Epilogue

## Sean

As the grandson of Holocaust survivors and the son of an alcoholic mother in recovery, I am part of this story. But this book is not about my experience growing up in this family. From my point of view, this is a story of how the Holocaust affected my grandparents' view of the world, their smothering overprotectiveness, ever present lack of trust, fear of loss, and the unintended damage to my mother and those around her. Despite our hardships, our story has a happy ending.

If I were able to speak to my grandparents now, I would say, "Thank you." During my tumultuous childhood, as my mother struggled with alcoholism, they became everything to me. They filled every role that I needed: teacher, parent, friend. In spite of the chaos and sadness in my mother's and my life, they kept us on life support.

My grandparents were involved in every area of parenting me, helping my mother when she wasn't able to. They brought their caretaking, love, and nurturing to our home. Although their overprotectiveness may not have been good for my mother, it was what I needed. I believe that despite the circumstances, they derived pleasure from helping us; it gave them a purpose. They took responsibility for us and never resented it, never complained, and were totally devoted.

Because my mother worked full-time and didn't arrive home until 6 or 6:30 p.m., my grandparents came to our apartment to keep me company after school. When they were in their sixties and seventies, they took the F train from Queens to Manhattan a couple of times a week, carrying bags of food they had prepared for us They enjoyed cooking and thought they would help out with dinner by bringing us meals that they had lovingly prepared. Feeding us gave them pleasure, and they wanted to make the dinner hour easier for my mother after her long day at work. They even helped with the laundry on occasion.

I became very close with my grandparents because I spent so much time with them and got to know them well. They provided me with a sense of stability and security. They were both wonderful people but differed in their approach to life; yesterday formed my grandmother's opinions, while tomorrow formed my grandfather's. Grandma seemed to hold on to fear, anger, and resentment, whereas Grandpa was the eternal optimist. Although he remembered everything he went through during the Holocaust and was scarred by it, he was able to move forward. Despite those differences, both of them had a positive effect on me.

My grandfather was a powerful example for me as I was growing up. When I needed someone to set me straight, to help me cope, my grandfather stepped in. On weekends, when I went to my grandparents' house, he guided me to develop a vocabulary by reading newspapers. He made sure that I wasn't failing at school and instructed me in various subjects like math and history.

Grandma helped create a safe haven for me to express my thoughts during the most tumultuous times of my young life. I have fond memories of the weekends when I stayed at their house. I had my own room to sleep in, but after dinner I liked watching television in my grandparents' bedroom, sitting on my grandmother's bed. As a treat, they used to bring me an English muffin or a piece of cake. The time I looked forward to most was when Grandma and I spent time together talking about friends, what was going on at home, stories of the war, sports, everything. We became very close.

If I could speak to my grandparents now, I would also apologize to them. I'm sorry for what I put them through during my rebellious teenage years because they must have been terrified. Not only did they have to take care of my mother, but they also had to take care of me. I understand that they may have made mistakes raising my mother, but they couldn't help it. Their experiences during the Holocaust affected their belief system and outlook on life. But I forgive them. Because of them, I strive to be the good of what they were.

While my grandparents' stories are part of my family's history and serve as a record of their experience, the most remarkable story for me is my mother's survival journey from alcohol addiction to recovery. Growing up with parents who had been severely scarred by their Holocaust experience couldn't have been easy for her. The first three years of her life in the Bergen-Belsen displaced persons camp, living among survivors who were dealing with their own trauma and loss, did not provide an ideal environment for a carefree childhood. The fear and anxiety transmitted to her continued when my mother and my grandparents came to the United States. My mother told me that as a child, she thought that it was normal to feel fearful and worried, but she didn't understand how those emotions were affecting her. She said, "I found it unbearable to live in my own skin." Left on her own to cope without the possibility of outside help, it's not surprising that when my mother had her first experience with alcohol as a young teenager, she felt a temporary relief from her anxiety.

I witnessed her struggle with alcohol over the years, and, of course, I was impacted by it in many ways, but one of the beautiful things about my mother was that as I was growing up, while she realized that she was struggling and couldn't help herself, she knew that I was troubled and insisted I go to Alateen and later got me my own therapist. She always says that God used me, her only joy and meaning in life, to have the strength to say, "I'm done."

In recovery, my mother has made living amends to our family through her behavior and her actions. Living amends involves improving relationships and giving of yourself. As she describes it, "Continue to rise to your best life to the people you have harmed." My mother was totally devoted to her parents in their later years by spending time with them, accompanying them to their doctor's appointments, doing their food shopping, and running errands.

Instead of looking back on what happened and what could have been, I am more focused on where we are now. The contrast between the past and today is incredible. It's a relief for me that I no longer spend part of my day wondering what's going on with my mother, a weight that I carried for much of my life. Those days are gone.

I am joyful that she has discovered and continues her path of spiritual awakening and recovery. As a result, our relationship is strong. My family has the benefit of her living close by so that we can help each other and share family time. She can enjoy being a grandmother to my son and daughter and participate in their lives. They, in turn, have the opportunity to get to know her and enjoy spending one-on-one time with her. I get to feel the joy that she is finally happy. This is everything to me because this is what I want for her.

Our story has a happy ending. I know that my grandparents were finally able to experience glimmers of sunshine towards the end of their lives, and my mother's dark, hopeless days are gone.